CONTEMPORARY AMERICAN MONOLOGUES FOR WOMEN

CONTEMPORARY AMERICAN MONOLOGUES FOR WOMEN

EDITED BY TODD LONDON

THEATRE COMMUNICATIONS GROUP

Copyright © 1998 by Theatre Communications Group, Inc.

Introduction, "An Actor Chooses," and monologue introductions copyright © 1998 by Todd London.

Contemporary American Monologues for Women is published by Theatre Communications Group, Inc., 520 Eighth Ave., 24th Fl., New York, NY 10018–4156.

This publication is made possible in part with public funds from the New York State Council on the Arts, a State Agency.

TCG books are exclusively distributed to the book trade by Consortium Book Sales and Distribution, 1045 Westgate Dr., St. Paul, MN 55114.

Library of Congress Cataloging-in-Publication Data

Contemporary American monologues for women / Todd London, editor.
—1st ed.
p.   cm.
Includes bibliographical references.
ISBN-13: 978-1–55936–133–0
ISBN-10: 1–55936–133–6 (alk. paper)
1. Acting—Auditions.   2. Monologues.   3. American drama—20th century.
4. Women—drama. I. London, Todd.
PN2080.C646   1997
812'.04508'082–dc21   97–5737
                                                                                                          CIP

Cover design by Paula Scher
Book design and composition by Lisa Govan

First Edition, January 1998
Eighth Printing, December 2006

ACKNOWLEDGMENTS

The playwrights whose words appear in this volume are, of course, its authors. They have been consistently encouraging, generous and remarkably tolerant of the piecework I've made of their art. I'm grateful to them all.

Special thanks to Nancy C. Jones, Kerry Lowe and Timothy Mennel, who did much of the hard labor on this book. Thanks, too, to Gino DiIorio, Nancy Piccione, the writers and staff of New Dramatists and, especially, Terry Nemeth.

My deepest appreciation goes, always, to Juanita and Guthrie.

Editor's note: Many of the monologues that follow have been cobbled together to make sense out of context. Where lines of dialogue or stage directions have been cut, three open boxes—□□□—mark the deletion.

CONTENTS

INTRODUCTION

This collection has a simple aim: to make matches. You're an actor searching for the right monologue—for auditions or acting class—and here are cuttings from dozens of the most exciting American plays of the past two decades. The material might be said to be searching, too. It's on the lookout for actors who will connect deeply, who have the emotional availability and the craft to deliver these monologues into the world with their complexity intact. It seeks actors who think on their feet, who understand in their bodies the impression contemporary life makes on a character. Like any matchmaker, though, this book offers only an introduction. The work is left to you.

Some of the excerpts collected here will read like nothing else you've found. Some are more difficult than others, some more strange, but they all offer a freshness of voice, an originality that can only be fully felt/heard/appreciated in context. So, I encourage you, once you've discovered a monologue you like (or two or ten), to read the complete play. (In the interview that follows, Nancy Piccione, one of New York's most respected and experienced casting directors, offers the same advice.) They're all published and easy to lay hands on.

This volume gathers solos from well-made plays, autobiographical performances, experimental playwriting and unabashedly political theatre. Often, these scripts mix dramatic or tragic tones with comic and farcical ones—even in the same monologue. Thematically, too, while many of these writers tackle matters of life and death, love and loss—themes with great traditions in the theatre—they also go where plays haven't gone in quite the same ways before. Racial identity, female sexuality, political domination, psychobabble, food art, age, evil, AIDS, motherhood, life after death—it's all here, dished up with fierce intelligence and terrific wit. You can't make rich sense of any of it from a single speech.

This book assumes not only that you love to act but also that you love to read plays. That's one of the reasons it's divided into named chapters instead of into more standard categories, such as age

range, or dramatic and comic. Also, more than a few of these monologues can be played in a variety of ways by a variety of "types" of
actors. As mentioned above, the sensibilities of contemporary playwriting make it harder, too, to classify works as "comic" or "dramatic." Is a paranoid teenager afraid of a garbage disposal merely funny?
What about a psychologist who gouges her eyes out when her last
patient quits therapy or a semiliterate girl who mangles Shakespeare's
poetry even as it seeps into her heart?

These monologues are grouped (and the groups titled) with the
hope of sparking an immediate connection. They're organized by
subject (women and food, life with men, artistic aspiration), by emotional impulse ("I thought my heart would burst") and by action
("Dreaming ahead"). Some headings are designed to suggest a common thread of character or predicament—"Why don't you talk to a
psychiatrist?" for example. You might want to thumb through the
book the way you would an anthology of short stories or poems, until
one piece grabs you and inspires you to try it out. Or, if you need
information about age and character type right off the bat, go
straight to the introductory paragraphs, and they'll tell you what you
need to know. There's a range of women's experience represented
here, for actors of every age, temperament and ethnic background,
actors of every stamp.

This book has another aim, too, shared by its publisher, Theatre
Communications Group, from whose playlist these brave new works
are culled. That goal is to get new American plays out into the world.
For this mission, too, the interests of actors and playwrights overlap.
Actors need words, and writers need real voices for their interior
ones; you need compelling roles, and they need disciplined, resilient
actors to breathe stage life into their characters. Both want to make
thrilling, important theatre. Neither can do so without the other. It's
a natural match.

—T. L.

AN ACTOR CHOOSES

AN INTERVIEW WITH NANCY PICCIONE

Since 1992, Nancy Piccione has been director of casting for Manhattan Theatre Club and casting consultant for the American Repertory Theatre in Cambridge, Massachusetts. Before that, she handled casting for the New York Shakespeare Festival for ten years, seven of those as casting director. Her extensive work with new plays and Shakespeare has been seen on and off Broadway.

What should an actor look for in audition material?

General auditions are probably the hardest auditions to do, since they're not for a specific role and they are memorized. An actress has to look for material that will show her range of skills in all of three minutes to six minutes. What matters is that she feels connected to it and feels comfortable with it.

How should actors use these few minutes? What do you as a casting director want to see? Should they concern themselves with character, the way they would in a full-length play? Or should they try to reveal something of themselves? Are auditions about how they play an action or about what their emotional range is?

I think auditioning is more about the action and the emotional range than about themselves because, simply, that's what acting is: transformation. Also, in any list of monologues there are degrees of difficulty—just like in the Olympic diving competitions. In a way, that's what they're showing more than themselves, the level of skill. But they must also demonstrate an emotional connection to the material. We don't need to see emotional breakdowns; there's not enough time, given the confines of a three-minute monologue, to build that up. It's more valuable to communicate texture and levels of. . . . What's the perfect word for this? It's funny, because sometimes you'll see someone do a monologue and you'll say, "There's a lot of *stuff* going on. Got a lot of stuff there." It's a funny word, but it describes the feeling of being able to see that an actor is thinking, feeling, talking and physicalizing convincingly as a character.

Can you define "stuff"?

The first definition of "stuff" is truthfulness. When you say a performance is very truthful, it means that the actor has connected with the role and completely transformed into that character, that she's traveling the character's emotional journey. Stuff also includes technique.

What is technique?

Technique incorporates training and experience. The actor knows how to approach the monologue from a technical viewpoint—the way a musician would approach a piece of music—knows she can play the right notes and then bring other emotional and psychological levels to it. That's what I mean by stuff, then: truthfulness, technique and, back to the heart, emotional connection.

I've seen actors give strong, memorable auditions by doing something very simply. You talk about emotional range, and I wonder about simplicity, because actors can feel the need to pump up what they do.

Truthfulness is the main thing; that's where simplicity comes in. No matter how complex a role, if you keep it simple and truthful, it will probably come off better than if you overact or overdramatize.

So the choice of material is less about a role you would be able to play than about being able to show your stuff?

I wouldn't say that. It should also be a role you'd be able to play.

Do you mean a role you'd be able to play at this point in your life?

That's usually the wisest choice. That doesn't mean you can't play other things, but open-call auditions boil down to who can come in the room and give the quickest demonstration of their talent. The actor needs to take that into her own hands and, for her own marketability, cast herself as somebody close to her.

Do you have any practical suggestions?

I do, but they're just my feelings; they're purely subjective, and another casting director might tell you the exact opposite. To me, it's important that an actor understands the play because I want to see the monologue performed in the context of what the play is about. If an actress is doing the "quality of mercy" speech from *Merchant of Venice*, for example, and doesn't know where it's taking place and when it's taking place and why, she won't bring as much richness to her performance. Or if it's Paula Vogel's *The Baltimore Waltz*, it's important to know that the woman's brother died of AIDS. Performing something within its whole context, portraying the character in that moment of the play, shows more skill.

So, read the play completely. In an audition room, somebody might ask you about it, and the worst thing you could say is, "Oh, I don't know the play. I just know the monologue."

Any other practical things?

I'd say don't bring props in. Another: I don't think it's wise to do original material, material you've written. The minute I know that's what I'm watching, I'm considering the writing as well as the acting. It can be hard to separate the two.

And you have to be able to adjust to any physical space. I've held auditions in big theatres and little theatres, tiny little screening rooms. Sometimes people hold auditions in offices. You have to go with whatever the space may be, and you're not going to know until you walk in the room. If you're going to lie down on the floor for most of your monologue—

—Make sure their desk isn't in the way.

Yes. Other practical suggestions: I feel it's important to look nice. I don't mean fancy; jeans and a T-shirt can look nice if they're fresh and clean. It helps the actor. I remember doing a general audition once where the actress came in barefoot. Now, there's nothing wrong with that, but I had no clue why, so it distracted me from watching the actor.

What about using the other people in the room?

You should ask if you can use them and be prepared that they might say no. I prefer not to be used because I have to take notes as I go. I look up and down and up and down, and I'm just not helpful to them.

If the actor doesn't use an actual person, where should she place the imaginary one she's speaking to?

I think it works to focus over the heads of the auditors, so they can see all of you, not to audition off toward stage left or stage right, to perform in profile. I want to see all of you.

What goes through your head when you're watching somebody?

First, I'm getting a physical picture. Second, I'm watching for truth and simplicity. If I know the play really well, I'm looking for a connection to the character at that moment in the play. I'm thinking about comedic ability and dramatic strength and listening for clarity of language—always. I'm also looking for what we call "centeredness," when a person is centered in the moment. As casting directors we do look for that, and we sense it.

I don't want to be negative in an audition. What actors have to do is horrible; auditioning is a terrible process. I wish we could figure out a better way to do it. And I'm very much on the side of the actor. I will defend actors to the nth degree, to the final hour. I really want, when people come into the room, for them to be good.

Let's go back to what you called "degree of difficulty." The term suggests that in casting you enjoy seeing people rise to the challenge of the material.

Definitely. It's simpler to find clear examples in Shakespeare than in contemporary work because people know those characters. Hamlet's speech, "O, what a rogue and peasant slave am I!" is a far higher degree of difficulty than Puck's "If we shadows have offended," from *A Midsummer Night's Dream*. Think of the situation, the context in which the monologues appear. Look at what Hamlet's going through emotionally when he says that speech. Puck, at the end of the play, is in a much easier situation than Hamlet.

So, you're saying that there are moments in a play of emotional or intellectual duress, a test or crucible. The character is right there down and center where everything they are is called upon. Then there are other, less dramatically difficult moments, even within the same play, where the character is narrating or retelling or in the process of figuring something out.

Exactly. Here's another example: In *Twelfth Night*, Malvolio's yellow-garter speech is probably much more difficult than Olivia's speech after Viola leaves. Malvolio performs a play within the play in that monologue; he goes through a million emotions. It's funny and sad at the same time. Olivia's just talking to herself about what she's just felt.

There are minds at work in today's theatre, too, that seem to revel in providing actors with these challenges. I'm thinking, for example, of Nicky Silver's witty, panicked high-wire acts, the way he creates the most extreme circumstances for his characters and forces them to deal; or the way Tony Kushner's characters think and feel at the same exuberant pitch; the challenging riffs of language in Suzan-Lori Parks's work or of meaning in Richard Foreman. Even the emotional journeys in a play like Paula Vogel's *How I Learned to Drive*—these are tortuous, difficult journeys, written in that clean, smart style.

Absolutely. That's why it's important to choose monologues that will show your particular strengths. I want to say one final thing about degree of difficulty, though: it's better to pick something easier that you can do well than to bite off more than you can chew and do something that's too difficult for you.

It's really basic. You're going for a complete connection to a character you understand inside and out. You want to feel confident that you can do what the character needs to do within that three minutes. You want to feel competent, secure in your talent, that you can do this audition in any situation anywhere. Your audition is your calling card.

"LISTEN TO YOUR NIGHTMARES"

A BRIGHT ROOM CALLED DAY

BY TONY KUSHNER

Zillah Katz is out of time with the play around her: it unfolds in Weimar Germany in the early thirties; she is alone in America, talking to the audience, circa 1990. In her "completely convinced, humorless, paranoic" mind, however, the Hitler years and those of Reagan and Bush are connected, as they're both times of ascendant evil. In the author's words, Zillah's a "contemporary American Jewish woman. 30s. BoHo/East Village New Wave with Anarcho-Punk tendencies." When she's not exhorting the audience, she's obsessively firing off letters to the powers of evil.

ZILLAH: German lessons. Listen:
"Das Massengrab." Mass grave.
"Die Zeit war sehr schlimm." Times were bad.
"Millionen von Menschen waren tot." Millions of people were dead.
People try to be so fussy and particular when they look at politics, but what I think an understanding of the second half of the twentieth century calls for is not caution and circumspection but moral exuberance. Overstatement is your friend: use it. Take Evil: The problem is that we have this event—Germany, Hitler, the Holocaust—which we have made into THE standard of absolute Evil—well and good, as standards of Evil go, it's not bad—but then everyone gets frantic as soon as you try to use the standard, *nothing* compares, *nothing* resembles—and the standard becomes unusable and *nothing* qualifies as Evil with a capital E. I mean how much of a Nazi do you have to be to qualify for membership? Is a twenty-five-percent Nazi a Nazi or not? Ask yourselves this: it's 1942; the Goerings are having an intimate soiree; if he got an invitation, would Pat Buchanan feel out of place? Out of place? Are you *kidding*? Pig *heaven*, dust off the old tuxedo, kisses to Eva and Adolf. I mean just because a certain ex-actor-turned-President who shall go nameles sat *idly* by and watched tens of thousands die of a plague and he couldn't even bother to say

he felt *bad* about it, much less try to *help*, does this mean he merits comparison to a certain fascist-dictator anti-Semitic mass-murdering psychopath who shall also remain nameless? OF COURSE NOT! I mean I ask you—how come the only people who ever say "Evil" anymore are southern cracker televangelists with radioactive blue eyeshadow? None of these bastards *look* like Hitler, they never will, not exactly, but I say as long as they look like they're playing in Mr. Hitler's Neighborhood we got no reason to relax.

I never relax. I can work up a sweat reading the Sunday *Times*. I read, I gasp, I hit the streets at three a.m. with my can of spray paint: REAGAN EQUALS HITLER! RESIST! DON'T FORGET, WEIMAR HAD A CONSTITUTION TOO!

Moral exuberance. Hallucination, revelation, gut-flutters in the night—the internal intestinal night bats, their panicky leathery wings—that's my common sense. I pay attention to that. Don't put too much stock in a good night's sleep. During times of reactionary backlash, the only people sleeping soundly are the guys who're giving the rest of us bad dreams. So eat something indigestible before you go to bed, and listen to your nightmares.

A BRIGHT ROOM CALLED DAY

BY TONY KUSHNER

ZILLAH:
Dear Mr. President,
I know you will never read this letter. I'm fully aware of the fact that letters to you don't even make it to the White House, that they're brought to an office building in Maryland where civil-servant types are paid to answer the sane ones. Crazy, hostile letters—like mine— the ones written in crayon on butcher paper, the ones made of letters cut out of magazines—these get sent to the FBI, analyzed, Xeroxed and burned. But I send them anyway, once a day, and do you know why? Because the loathing I pour into these pages is so ripe, so full-to-bursting, that it is my firm belief that anyone touching them will absorb into their hands some of the toxic energy contained

therein. This toxin will be passed upwards—it is the nature of bureau-cracies to pass things vertically—till eventually, through a network of handshakes, the Under-Secretary of Outrageous Falsehoods will shake hands with the Secretary for Pernicious Behavior under the Cloak of Night, who will, on a weekly basis in Cabinet meetings, shake hands with you before you nod off to sleep. In this way, through osmosis, little droplets of contagion are being rubbed into your leath-ery flesh every day—in this great country of ours there must be thou-sands of people who are sending you poisoned post. We wait for the day when all the grams and drams and dollops of detestation will destroy you. We attack from below. Our day will come. You can try to stop me. You can raise the price of stamps again. I'll continue to write. I'm saving up for a word processor. For me and my cause, money is no object.

Love,
Zillah.

MARISOL

BY JOSÉ RIVERA

In present-day New York City, the world has turned violent, terrifying, unrecognizable. Apples are extinct, the color blue has disappeared from the sky, cows' milk has gone salty, and no one has seen the moon in nine months. An angel appears in this nightmare landscape, "a young black woman in ripped jeans, sneakers, and black T-shirt. Crude silver wings hang limply from the back of Angel's diamond-studded leather jacket." She has, until now, been guardian angel to Marisol Perez of the Bronx and, as she details below, saved Marisol's life many times. She's giving up her charge, though, in order to lead the angels' revolution against God. He's the one, she claims, who's brought the world to ruin. She's talking to the sleeping Marisol.

ANGEL: I kick-started your heart, Marisol. I wired your nervous sys-tem. I pushed your fetal blood in the right direction and turned the foam in your infant lungs to oxygen. When you were six and your parents were fighting, I helped you pretend you were underwater: that you were a cold-blooded fish, in the bottom of the black ocean, far away and safe. When racists ran you out of school at ten, screaming □□□ I turned the monsters into little columns of salt! At last count, one plane crash, one collapsed elevator, one massacre at the hands of a right-wing fanatic with an Uzi, and sixty-six-thousand-six-hundred-and-three separate sexual assaults never happened because of me. □□□ Now the bad news. □□□

I can't expect you to understand the political ins and outs of what's going on. But you have eyes. You asked me questions about children and water and war and the moon: the same questions I've been asking myself for a thousand years. □□□

The universal body is sick, Marisol. Constellations are wasting away, the nauseous stars are full of blisters and sores, the infected earth is running a temperature, and everywhere the universal mind is wracked with amnesia, boredom, and neurotic obsessions. □□□ Because God is old and dying and taking the rest of us with Him. And for too long, much too long, I've been looking the other way. Trying to stop the massive hemorrhage with my little hands, with my prayers. But it didn't work and I knew if I didn't do something soon, it would be too late. □□□ I called a meeting. And I urged the Heavenly Hierarchies—the Seraphim, Cherubim, Thrones, Dominions, Principalities, Powers, Virtues, Archangels and Angels—to vote to stop the universal ruin . . . by slaughtering our senile God. And they did. Listen well, Marisol: angels are going to kill the King of Heaven and restore the vitality of the universe with His blood. And I'm going to lead them.

FAT MEN IN SKIRTS

BY NICKY SILVER

Phyllis Hogan, "an attractive and sophisticated woman in her 40s," has just, following the crash of her plane, been stranded on a deserted island with her strange son, Bishop. Everyone else has died. When Bishop complains that he's starving, she sends him after the only food on the island. "Here's a knife," she says. "Go back to the plane and cut the arm off that nun. Bring it back here and I'll cook it and we'll eat it." He returns holding the nun's arm—still clutching a rosary— triumphantly aloft. She steps toward the audience and speaks.

PHYLLIS: Lately, I have been having a recurring dream. When I was a little girl, we lived in a part of Philadelphia called Society Hill. In an apartment. Down the hall from us lived a Mr. Antonelli. Mr. Antonelli worked at the Museum of Natural History. And he was big. He was a big man. Must've weighed three hundred pounds. He was the fattest human being I'd ever seen, close up. But he was well-groomed. And on certain nights of the week, Saturdays, I think, Saturdays mostly and Thursdays, Mr. Antonelli would dress as a woman and go wherever three-hundred-pound men who dress as women go, to seek whatever they can mistake for love. He'd put on a skirt and a blouse, sometimes a mumu-Bloody-Mary-type thing. And a lot of makeup. He wore a wig, a reddish kind of Ethel Merman affair. And always lovely matching jewelry sets: green rhinestone earrings, green rhinestone bracelets, brooches. He got all dolled up and went off to seek others like himself (although I can't imagine there were many others like Mr. Antonelli; three-hundred-pound transvestites are pretty much on their own in the world, I should think). When I was six, I was going to a friend's birthday party on Saturday, and I was wearing the sweetest little powder-blue jumper, and Mr. Antonelli got into the elevator with my mother and me. He looked down at me—this great mountain of gelatinous white flesh, and said, "My goodness, what a sweet little blue dress you have on." And I said, "You could borrow it sometime, if you want, Mr. Antonelli." I was six, and the concept of Junior and Misses sizing had not yet been made clear to me. Well, my mother squeezed my hand so tightly I thought my fingers would snap off. Once on the street, she explained to me that I must never, ever speak to Mr. Antonelli again. If he spoke to me, I was to nod politely. But I was never—under any circumstances—to speak to him again. And I was certainly not to get into the elevator with him. My mother explained to me that Mr. Antonelli was a freak. That he should be locked up. Forgotten about. That Mr. Antonelli, although not to blame him for his condition, was nevertheless, the lowest form of the species, a creature to fear, and his parents, poor souls, must have a terrible burden to bear. Now. In my dream, I'm a little girl again. And I'm wearing my little powder-blue jumper. The one I wore that day. Only, I'm not on my way to any birthday party. I'm on a field trip with my class from school. We're at the zoo. Riding the monorail and laughing. The sun is shining, balloons fill the sky and we have cotton candy for lunch. We go to the reptile house and the polar-bear cage and the tigers are sunning themselves. Then we go to the monkey house. But there aren't any monkeys. There are, climbing the jungle gym, picking salt from their hair, dozens and dozens of fat men in skirts. Huge fat men, with matching jewelry sets, swinging from limb to limb, laughing in no language. And everyone laughs and points. And then they turn around. All the monkeys. All the men turn around at once. They turn around and look at me, right at me. And they all have the same face. And it's Bishop's face. They all have my son's face.

TENEMENT LOVER:
No Palm Trees/In New York City

BY JESSICA HAGEDORN

The narrator's monologue is one of several self-contained stories in Jessica Hagedorn's multilayered performance piece. The play combines these stories with narrative fragments, images, music and visuals, as it intercuts scenes from the Philippines with scenes from Filipino life in New York. What we know about the character of the narrator is what she tells us here.

HER DEEPEST FEARS: THE NARRATOR'S MONOLOGUE: When I go home, back to the islands and my father's house, the same movie keeps unfolding in my head. They come and kill everyone in the house, and I'll just happen to be there. By chance, I tell myself. Except I know it's all part of my destiny. *(Pause)* There are three bedrooms in my father's house. My grandmother, paralyzed from a stroke, sleeps in the first bedroom at the top of the stairs. She is totally helpless, so a nurse remains at her side twenty-four hours a day. Socorro is fed intravenously, and shits into a sack that's attached to her side. Socorro clutches a rosary in her gnarled hands and mumbles to herself. No one can make out what she's saying. Socorro's eyes are glazed, she sits in her wheelchair and trembles ever so slightly . . . I imagine she's already left her body, that she exists on some high spiritual plane. *(Pause)* In my movie, they kill the nurse first. They never touch my grandmother. In fact, they seem to be afraid of her. After the massacre, she's the only survivor left—mumbling in her wheelchair and clutching the rosary beads in her disfigured hands. *(Pause)* I sleep in the second bedroom. I hear them kill the nurse, quietly and efficiently. She makes one low sound. I lie in my bed, sweating, staring at the door. I hear the leaves rustling outside the screened window—the night is humming, alive with cicadas chirping and clicking. It is unbearably hot, even in the middle of the night. I am unable to move, sweating under my thin blanket. I hear soft movements in the next room. They are coming for me, I am sure of it. I go over the movie again and again, the movie I call *My Father's House. (Pause)* I often imagine the face of my killer. He is a feline guerrilla, with sharp cheekbones, copper skin, and blue-black hair. His sharp eyes pierce the darkness; he carefully bends his sullen face towards mine. My father sleeps in the third bedroom. *(Pause)* For a brief moment, I am sure the young man is actually going to kiss me. But I am wrong.

2

"MY LIFE WITH HIM"

THE MODERN LADIES
OF GUANABACOA

BY EDUARDO MACHADO

*1928. An attractive woman in her late forties, Maria Josefa is the
matriarch of a prosperous Cuban family. She is devoted to her husband, Arturo, and her sons and serves them according to clearly
articulated codes of behavior. She painstakingly teaches her daughter, Manuela, these codes. Keeping up with modern times—in this
case cutting their hair—requires Arturo's permission. Maintaining
custom has also, until now, required blindness to his philandering,
Arturo's status as "the greatest stud in the province of Havana."
Maria Josefa has just learned about his other life, though—an affair
with an American woman—and confronted him. She swears never to
touch him again or even to look at him. In a moment of rebellion—
a change in the fixed order—she tells him she is cutting her hair, and
he reasserts his authority by giving permission. He exits. She speaks
alone onstage.*

MARIA JOSEFA: I did the job twelve times. Arturo de la Asuncion Ripoll
born July 16, 1895. Died at birth. Ernesto born June 7, 1898.
Manuela born January 1, 1901, she grew up to be his true love.
Mario born December 22, 1906. Fernando de la Asuncion Ripoll
born July 23, 1909, died October 30, 1907. Gilda de la Asuncion
Ripoll born May 29, 1909, died June 10, 1909, Miguel born March
10, 1911, Pepe de la Asuncion Ripoll born March 7, 1912, died four
months later, Antonia de la Asuncion Ripoll born April 22, 1913, died
December 23, 1913, all the babies that went from the womb to the
breast to the grave. I had no milk, so they died. Olga de la Asuncion
Ripoll born November 18, 1915, born dead, and the one that was
early and died the next day, Eurgenio de la Asuncion Ripoll. Enrique
born November 14, 1902. Died aged eleven, December 26, 1913.
There was something wrong with his blood. That is my life with him
and he talks about discretion. *(She gets scissors)* Manuela dear,

wake up. Father gave us his permission. We're cutting our hair. We are going to be in style, dear.

RECKLESS

BY CRAIG LUCAS

Pooty, a paraplegic in a wheelchair, lives with Lloyd, the man she loves. Lloyd, who thinks she's not only crippled but also deaf and mute, loves her back. Here, several scenes into the play, she speaks for the first time. She tells her story—to Rachel, a stranger, who arrived at their house on Christmas Eve wearing a nightgown and slippers—and stops a split second before Lloyd walks in.

POOTY: When I lost the use of my legs a friend drove me up here to Springfield to take a look at this place where they worked with the handicapped. I watched the physical therapists working with the patients and there was one: I remember he was working with a quadriplegic. I thought he was the most beautiful man I'd ever seen. A light shining out through his skin. And I thought if I couldn't be with him I'd die. But I knew I would just be one more crippled dame as far as he was concerned, so my friend helped to get me registered as deaf and disabled. I used to teach sign language to the hearing impaired. I thought if I were somehow needier than the rest I would get special attention. I realized soon enough: everyone gets special attention where Lloyd is concerned. But by then it was too late. He was in love with me, with my honesty. He learned to sign; he told me how he'd run away from a bad marriage and changed his name so he wouldn't have to pay child support. He got me a job at Hands Across the Sea and I couldn't bring myself to tell him that I had another name and another life, that I'd run away too, because I owed the government so much money and wasn't able to pay after the accident. I believe in honesty. I believe in total honesty. And I need him and he needs me to be the person he thinks I am and I am that person, I really am that person. I'm a crippled deaf girl, short and stout. Here is my wheelchair, here is my mouth. □□□ When he goes out I babble. I recite poetry I remember from grade school. I talk back to the television. I even call people on the phone and say it's a wrong number just to have a conversation. I'm afraid I'm going to open my mouth to scream one day and . . . *(She does; no sound)*

THREE HOTELS

BY JON ROBIN BAITZ

Alone in a hotel room, Barbara Hoyle, a corporate wife now dressed in "T-shirt, old jeans, and sneakers," tells her story to the audience. Her husband, who once worked with her in the Peace Corps, is a rising vice president for a multinational business that markets baby formula to the Third World. Their relationship has grown strained over the years as he's hardened into the role of corporate hatchet man. Last year, their son Brandon was stabbed to death on a beach in Brazil, days before they were to return to the States. The speech she describes is the very thing the corporate wives never expect to hear; it will have the effect of bringing her husband's career to an end.

BARBARA: My speech to young wives assigned to the Third World—the 3-W club, they call it—they have a little newsletter. I used to even write for it now and then when we were in Brazil. Mostly recipes—that's all they wanted really was mostly recipes and shopping hints. *(Beat)* My speech was entitled BE CAREFUL. Simply BE CAREFUL. ☐☐☐ I say this to them and I mean it, I want to help. "Be careful of spending too much time alone. Learn the language—whatever you do—learn the language fast. The silence in those houses they find for you with the servants—it can overwhelm you." I smile. A sister. "Look. I'm gonna level with you,"—now I know I'm really hitting my stride, doing a sort of a midwife routine—"they say it's an adventure and it is. But it's also a sacrifice. You're giving up things here and when you come back, it'll never be the same—make sure your husband understands this. Make sure he knows that what you're coming back to is not the . . ."
(Pause)

"Of course, not all of you will come back with a dead son."
(Beat. She smiles sadly)
Have I crossed a line? I never talk about this. But it seems false—
mealymouthed not to make mention of it—and I—to tell you the
truth—I am beginning to realize it is expected of me.

I go on. "Most likely, percentage-wise very few of you will come back
without a child—but if you do . . . come back . . . with a coffin . . .
(Beat)
"Talk about it." They nod. They *know*. They're women for God's sake,
not just DARs. I shake my head. "You know—we hear the news. 'We're
moving overseas.' Maybe we're sitting in the kitchen alone after
they've gone to the office, having that quiet cup of afternoon coffee
and the phone rings and it's your husband and he says, 'I was right.
We're going to . . . Surinam or Sri Lanka or *Rio*.' And there is this sense
of . . . 'oh, it's a mission. . .' that sort of overtakes you. A dream.

"Remember, it is not . . . your mission. Your husband's mission is
not—your mission. Be careful . . . that you keep the clarity of your
own life." I pause. They are nodding. "Or you will come back and you
will have . . . dust. You will have nothing." Silence.

TALK RADIO

BY ERIC BOGOSIAN

*Linda MacArthur assistant-produces "Nighttalk" with Barry Cham-
plain on a talk-radio station in Cleveland, Ohio. Edgy, paranoid,
aggressive, belligerent and raw, the call-in show plays off the personality of its host, "an over-the-top, acerbic egomaniac," according
to the playwright. Here Linda serves up her own profile of Barry in
a monologue directed to the audience.*

LINDA: One night, after the show, I stopped by the lunchroom. I was
thirsty, I was gonna get a Coke out of the machine. Barry was there.
Sitting at the crummy table under the crummy fluorescent light. I didn't
know him. I had been working here two months and he had said
three words to me the whole time. He was sitting there staring at this

ashtray full of butts. Just sitting. I asked him if anything was wrong. . . .
He looked up at me like he'd never seen me before. Like he didn't
even know where he was. He said, "I'm outta cigarettes." I said,
"There's a machine down the hall. I'll get you some. . . ." I mean, he
coulda gotten the cigarettes himself, I know, but he seemed like he
couldn't at that moment. . . . He looked at me again and said, "Linda.
Can I go home with you tonight? Can I sleep with you?" Now, I've
had a lot of guys come on to me in a lot of ways. I expected this
Barry guy to have a smooth approach but this was unexpectedly
unique. I didn't say yes. I didn't say no. We went to this diner he likes
and I watched him eat a cheeseburger. He was talking about something, what was it? Euthanasia. I remember, because I thought, "This
guy really knows how to sweet-talk a girl." And the whole time smoking cigarettes, looking around, tapping his fingers. . . . Of course, we
ended up at my place. As I was getting us drinks, I said to myself,
"Linda, you know you're gonna go to bed with this guy, so let's get
the ball rolling." He was nervous, like he was gonna jump out of his
skin, so I started giving him a shoulder massage. The next thing,
we're on the floor and he's kissing me like he was in the middle of
the ocean, trying to get on a life raft! I got us into the bedroom . . .
and I go to the bathroom for two seconds to get myself together and
anyway, when I get back to the bed, he's asleep, curled up in a ball.
All that night, while he slept, he's throwing himself around, tossing
and turning, grinding his teeth, clenching his fists. It was scary. Next
morning, he's up before me. Comes out of the shower, he's a different guy. Says he never slept so well. Then he comes over to the bed
and . . . we made love. . . . Since then, we've spent maybe a dozen
nights together. . . . Lemme put it this way, Barry Champlain is a nice
place to visit, but I wouldn't want to live there.

HOW I LEARNED TO DRIVE

BY PAULA VOGEL

How I Learned to Drive *follows the obsession of Peck, a man in his*
forties, with his niece Li'l Bit—ages eleven to eighteen—and Li'l Bit's

fascination with him. Peck's wife, Mary, played by a member of the "Greek chorus," follows it, too. Whether she knows the full extent of their sexual secrets isn't clear; this, delivered to the audience, is all she'll say.

FEMALE GREEK CHORUS (AUNT MARY): My husband was such a good man—is. Is such a good man. Every night, he does the dishes. The second he comes home, he's taking out the garbage, or doing yard work, lifting the heavy things I can't. Everyone in the neighborhood borrows Peck—it's true—women with husbands of their own, men who just don't have Peck's abilities—there's always a knock on our door for a jump start on cold mornings, when anyone needs a ride, or help shoveling the sidewalk—I look out, and there Peck is, without a coat, pitching in.

I know I'm lucky. The man works from dawn to dusk. And the overtime he does every year—my poor sister. She sits every Christmas when I come to dinner with a new stole, or diamonds, or with the tickets to Bermuda.

I know he has troubles. And we don't talk about them. I wonder, sometimes, what happened to him during the war. The men who fought World War II didn't have "rap sessions" to talk about their feelings; they didn't break down and cry and protest. Men in his generation were expected to be quiet about it and get on with their lives. And sometimes I can feel him just fighting the trouble—whatever has burrowed deeper than the scar tissue—and we don't talk about it. I know he's having a bad spell because he comes looking for me in the house, and just hangs around me until it passes. And I keep my banter light—I discuss a new recipe, or sales, or gossip—because I think domesticity can be a balm for men when they're lost. We sit in the house and listen to the peace of the clock ticking in his well-ordered living room, until it passes.

(Sharply) I'm not a fool. I know what's going on. I wish you could feel how hard Peck fights against it—he's swimming against the tide, and what he needs is to see me on the shore, believing in him, knowing he won't go under, he won't give up—

And I want to say this about my niece. She's a sly one, that one is. She knows exactly what she's doing; she's twisted Peck around her little finger and thinks it's all a big secret. Yet another one who's borrowing my husband until it doesn't suit her anymore.

Well. I'm counting the days until she goes away to school. And she manipulates someone else. And then he'll come back again, and sit in the kitchen while I bake, or beside me on the sofa when I sew in the evenings. I'm a very patient woman. But I'd like him back

I am counting the days.

DESDEMONA

BY PAULA VOGEL

In this retelling of Othello, *Desdemona moonlights as a whore at Bianca's house for the sense of freedom it gives her. Her maid Emilia, on the other hand, described as a dark woman, "plump and plain, with a thick Irish brogue," lives as an honest, God-fearing woman and faithful wife, despite her husband's harsh treatment of her. At best, life offers Emilia the chance to plot and plan ways to earn a couple extra pennies a week and to get the man promoted, in hopes she'll end up "a lieutenant's widow." She speaks to Desdemona; they've just realized that one of Desdemona's johns, unrecognizable in the dark, was Emilia's husband, Iago.*

EMILIA: When I was married in the church, the knot tied beneath the Virgin's nose, I looked forward to the bed with as much joy as any girl after a hard day. And then Iago—well, he was still a lad, with the softness of a boy, and who could tell he'd turn into the man?

(Pauses to drink.)

But all that girl nonsense was knocked out of me by the nights. Night followin' night, as sure as the day's work came after. I'd stretch myself out on the bed, you see, waitin' for my good man to come to me and be my mate—as the priest said he could—but then . . . But then I saw it didn't matter what had gone on between us—the fights, my crying, a good meal or a cold one. Days could pass without a word between us, and he'd take his fill of me the same. I could have been the bed itself. And so, you see, I vowed not to be there for him. As he'd be lying on me in the dark, I'd picture up my Rosary, so real I could kiss the silver. And I'd start at the Blessed Cross itself, while he was somewhere doin' his business above, and I'd say the first wooden bead, and then I'd finger the next bead in my mind, and then onto the next—*(Stops)* But I never did make it to the medallion. He'd be all through with me by the time of the third "Hail Mary." □□□ Well, maybe it's all different for the likes of you. *(Desdemona says nothing)* And then, maybe not. It's hard to be seeing, when you're young and men watch you when you pass them by, and the talkin' stops between them. But, all in all, in time you'll know. Women just don't figure in their heads—not the one who hangs the wash—not Bianca—and not even you, m'lady. That's the hard truth. Men only see each other in their eyes. Only each other.

(Beat.)

And that's why I'm ready to leave the whole pack of them behind and go with you and the Ambassador. Oh, to see my husband's face tomorrow morning! When he finds out that I can get along by myself, with no thanks to his plotting and hatching! But it's leave him now or be countin' my beads through the years, waitin' for his last breath!

TENEMENT LOVER:
No Palm Trees/In New York City

BY JESSICA HAGEDORN

Tenement Lover is a performance piece that ties together self-contained stories, like the one below, with story fragments, images, music and visuals. Flashing from the Philippines to scenes of Filipino life in New York, the play reveals little about the characters beyond what's printed here. In "Ludivinda's Story," the twenty-four-year-old speaker watches television, "totally transfixed by the images. Occasionally, she munches on banana chips."

LUDIVINDA'S STORY: Tito was a marine . . . stationed at the base near where we lived. *(Pause)* We didn't know what a Puerto Rican was— it was funny when my family met him. *Ano ba iyan?* MENUDO? But Tito's American, I told them—something close to being Spanish, not dark at all. *I'm dark.* But Tito doesn't mind, he calls me beautiful. *(Pause)* Tito liked being in the marines. He says it's too hard in the outside world. But now with two kids, he can't go back in the marines—they keep telling him he's got too many dependents . . . *(Pause)* I'm twenty-four years old, and I'm glad we're off welfare. You should have seen our first apartment. Rats, roaches, the walls falling in. Are we in America? I asked my husband. *(Pause)* Once I worked as a clerk to help out with the family income. It made Tito so crazy! The only job he can get is as a security guard. We don't have a bank account because it isn't worth it—we keep taking out as soon as we put in. *(Pause)* Tito hated me working especially when he hadn't started his guard job and he had to stay home with the kids. "It's not right," he kept saying, "I don't feel like a man." I lost my job anyway, so it all worked out, I guess. *(Pause)* Tito's a good man— he doesn't drink or get high. He doesn't look at other women. One time I got angry with him. Only once. *(Pause)* We went to visit his friends in Brooklyn and I was feeling homesick. His friend's wife spoke Tagalog and asked me how come we never go dancing like they did. I got angry and asked Tito when we got home how come we never did that, dancing I mean—I love dancing, don't you? All Tito had to say was we better not see those people anymore because I was getting too jealous. *(Pause)* They were his only friends. *(Pause)* It's nice to have friends, but if they give you trouble I'd just as soon stay home . . . *(Pause)* We have two television sets, one in color. Tito watches sports games, but I like talk shows. Actually, I'll watch anything. So do the kids—we watch TV all day and all night, sometimes. *(Pause)* One of my real worries is that I'll never see my family back home again . . . and my parents will die and all this time will pass and I'll never have the money to go back . . . and this wavy black line, this black line that's been appearing on the bottom half of the screen of our color set . . . I can't call the repairman, we don't have any money, I just pretend the black line isn't there. Every day the black line gets worse, sometimes the pictures on the screen turn orange or pink, I think I'm going blind but no one else seems to notice. . . . Look, I tell my husband, it's going *bad*. It's on the *blink*. . . . What are we going to do? *(Pause)* Is okay, Tito tells me. Go watch the little set. I can't— I hate black-and-white TV—I keep telling Tito he should know this about me, I've told him many times, the same thing over and over again . . . *(Pause)* "Black-and-white's more realistic," he tells me, "you'll get used to it."

THE END OF THE DAY

BY JON ROBIN BAITZ

Helen Lasker-Massey's British-born husband has left her shortly after becoming a U.S. citizen. She arrives at his office thinking, "it might be productive, closure-wise, if we, clarification-wise, you know, kind of dealt with all of this 'cause I'm riding a major bummer." She admits to deep feeling but is not above threatening him. Baitz describes her as "a blowzy, attractive, smart blond."

HELEN: I drove down here to ask you a question. Something's been bothering me. Confusing me. When you upped and packed and walked out on me, I didn't say anything, you know? Slipping into wife-shock, nodding reasonably and letting you have your eloquent exit, Gray. □□□ Forgive me, sorry, forgive me, it's taken me a few days to get the balls to come down here and see you, but I am madly pissed-off here. □□□ The thing that has been bothering me, and we know I have these major-self-worth problems (you always reminded me), but you helped me. I lost thirty-nine pounds during our marriage. And dad, who has all the sensitivity of a cloven hoof, always made me feel dumb, and then you didn't, so I felt smart. But in retrospect, I was just taking your opinion of my intelligence on advisement, point being, in retrospect, that daddy was probably right. *(She smiles in apology, lips trembling. Controls herself)* Forgive me. This is a question I should've asked [when] you were packing your Asprey bags—for two days I've been gorging myself on granola and anchovy paste, so I'm having trouble expressing, but the big question—and it's a two-parter. *(Beat)* Did you ever think I was smart? □□□ Because I'm not. I'm not. I'm . . . gutter. I'm not clever, you—God, making me read. Me! Throwing your books at me! And paintings! And ugh . . . God. Taste. You and your good taste. *(Beat)* You took me down with it, I couldn't talk, but—here's the second part of my question. □□□ Did you ever love me, Graydon? □□□ I need to know. Did you ever love and respect me? Did you learn anything from me? Did I give you succor and warmth? What were you thinking when you hid in my chest at night, scared? Were we partners together? Did you ever stop in the middle of the goddamn day, Graydon, and wonder what I was doing or feeling? *(Pause)* Because I replay this thing in my head here and what I get to is that this marriage was a sad and—and—and decorous little affair—and what offends me—is that I do not believe you have answered me. I've had the last ten years of my life revealed to me as an absolute disaster. *(Beat)* If you know how much I hate myself for having let you lie to me for so long, I hate myself so much that it cancels out even blaming you. Oh, Graydon. Because what I've come up with is so interesting. And it never occurred to me consciously until this morning when I was eating my pasta. What I think is this: *(Pause)* I think you married me so as to become an American citizen.

APRIL SNOW

BY ROMULUS LINNEY

Grady Gunn is a prominent fifty-eight-year-old writer whose major work includes books on French literary and historical women and whose personal life revolves around an erratic lesbian relationship. Her lover, Mona, has, more than once, gone back to her husband, presumably out of guilt over their nine-year-old son Fred. Here, Grady recounts the latest chapter—Mona's return—to one of her closest friends, a man she was married to, briefly, twenty-eight years before.

GRADY: Mona's come back to me □□□ For good. □□□ A month ago. Mona's twenty-eight now. Little Fred is nine. This week, there had to be a visit. So, there was. Doorbell rang. There was Fred, coat and tie, hair slicked down, looking angelic. Behind him stood Richard, the injured father, looking innocent. The little boy and I faced each other. "Hi, Grady, " he said. "Hi, Fred." "Mama here?" "Yep." "Bye, Dad." Richard left. Mona came out of my kitchen. "Hi, Mama," said Fred. "Am I in the maid's room again?" *(Pause)* In the morning, I got up first. How to work? Think clearly about Madame de Staël, Madame Récamier and Madame Krudener? Read Sainte-Beuve, oh, please! I studied a paragraph. Madame Krudener dying, floating down the Volga on a houseboat with her coffin by her side. She was ridiculous.

All my work confronted me like a coffin. My home felt like a tomb. I felt like a corpse, and I was afraid of Mona's child. *(Pause)* They got up, made breakfast. I worked, pretending diligence. They tiptoed past my study, shushing each other. Utter silence. I hollered. "Oh, come in!" They did. Both, staring. Fred and I smiled. Like this. God. Two hypocrites. I wondered why he didn't leap over the desk, grab my throat, and throttle me. It's what I wanted to do to him. But the little boy whose mother left his father for me, *again*, he didn't do that. He tried to talk, coughed, blew his nose, as wretched as I was. Then he said, "Can I watch TV in the bedroom?" I said, "Sure." He kissed me, and he went into the room where his mother and I sleep, and watched his cartoons. He's with us every other weekend now. He says he loves me. I believe him. I want to believe him. I must. Madame de Staël, Madame Récamier, Madame Krudener, all talk happily at once. I just take it down. I love Mona. I love Fred. I stay home now. I will give only six readings next year. Do you see?

3

"EVERYTHING IN ITS PLACE"

IMPERCEPTIBLE MUTABILITIES IN THE THIRD KINGDOM

BY SUZAN-LORI PARKS

The play tells us little about Verona, except that her name is also Veronica and that she's a euthanasia specialist for a veterinary hospital. Whether her statement, "Once there was uh me name Verona" means that there was once a separate Veronica isn't explicit, but Parks's characters live in a shifting or mutable reality (as Verona's diction changes here mid-monologue when she describes her younger self). For example, in her only other scene, Verona watches her favorite TV show, Wild Kingdom; *it's an episode she's seen several times before, but this time she notices that, unlike the other times she's seen it, the host, Marlin Perkins, turns up with a gun and starts killing the wild beasts. Although Parks never says so explicitly, it's clear from the context and language of the play that Verona is African American. The "Third Kingdom" of the title includes the two worlds of the African American—preslavery Africa and America from slavery on—as well as all the sea in between. The monologue below is a scene unto itself, Verona's last appearance. It takes place, inexplicably, at a podium.*

VERONA: I saw my first pictures of Africa on TV: Mutual of Omahas *Wild Kingdom*. The thirty-minute filler between Walt Disneys wonderful world and the CBS Evening News. It was a wonderful world: Marlin Perkins and Jim and their African guides. I was a junior guide and had a lifesize poster of Dr. Perkins sitting on a white Land Rover surrounded by wild things. Had me an 8 x 10 glossy of him too, signed, on my nightstand. Got my nightstand from Sears cause I had to have Marlin by my bed at night. Together we learned to differentiate African from Indian elephants the importance of hyenas in the wild funny looking trees on the slant—how do they stand up? Black folks with no clothes. Marlin loved and respected all the wild things. His guides took his English and turned it into the local lingo so that he could converse with the natives. Marlin even petted a rhino once.

He tagged the animals and put them into zoos for their own protection. He encouraged us to be kind to animals through his shining example. Once there was uh me name Verona: I got mommy n dad tuh get me uh black dog n named it I named it "Namib" after thuh African sands n swore tuh be nice tuh it only Namib refused tuh be trained n crapped in corners of our basement n got up on thuh sofa when we went out n Namib wouldnt listen tuh me like Marlins helpers listened tuh him Namib wouldnt look at me when I talked tuh him n when I said someuhn like "sit" he wouldnt n "come" made im go n when I tied him up in thuh front yard so that he could bite the postman when thuh postman came like uh good dog would he wouldnt even bark just smile n wag his tail so I would kick Namib when no one could see me cause I was sure I was very very sure that Namib told lies uhbout me behind my back and Namib chewed through his rope one day n bit me n run off. I have this job. I work at a veterinarian hospital. I'm a euthanasia specialist. Someone brought a stray dog in one day and I entered "black dog" in the black book and let her scream and whine and wag her tail and talk about me behind my back then I offered her the humane alternative. Wiped her out! I stayed late that night so that I could cut her open because I had to see I just had to see the heart of such a disagreeable domesticated thing. But no. Nothing different. Everything in its place. Do you know what that means? Everything in its place. Thats all.

THE CONDUCT OF LIFE

BY MARIA IRENE FORNES

A middle-aged, somewhat retarded servant is in the midst of wiping crumbs from the table. Her mistress has interrupted her and tried to engage her in a different project, possibly to do with reading and writing. "Let's do this," she says. Olimpia, the servant, refuses to be distracted.

OLIMPIA *(In a mumble)*: As soon as I finish doing this. You can't just ask me to do what you want me to do, and interrupt what I'm doing. I don't stop from the time I wake up in the morning to the time I go to sleep. You can't interrupt me whenever you want, not if you want me to get to the end of my work. I wake up at 5:30. I wash. I put on my clothes and make my bed. I go to the kitchen. I get the milk and the bread from outside and I put them on the counter. I open the icebox. I put one bottle in and take the butter out. I leave the other bottle on the counter. I shut the refrigerator door. I take the pan that I use for water and put water in it. I know how much. I put the pan on the stove, light the stove, cover it. I take the top off the milk and pour it in the milk pan except for a little. *(Indicating with her finger)* Like this. For the cat. I put the pan on the stove, light the stove. I put coffee in the thing. I know how much. I light the oven and put bread in it. I come here, get the tablecloth and I lay it on the table. I shout "Breakfast." I get the napkins. I take the cups, the saucers, and the silver out and set the table. I go to the kitchen. I put the tray on the counter, put the butter on the tray. The water and the milk are getting hot. I pick up the cat's dish. I wash it. I pour the milk I left in the bottle in the milk dish. I put it on the floor for the cat. I shout "Breakfast." The water boils. I pour it in the thing. When the milk boils I turn off the gas and cover the milk. I get the bread from the oven. I slice it down the middle and butter it. Then I cut it in pieces *(Indicating)* this big. I set a piece aside for me. I put the rest of the bread in the bread dish and shout "Breakfast." I pour the coffee in the coffee pot and the milk in the milk pitcher, except I leave *(Indicating)* this much for me. I put them on the tray and bring them here. If you're not in the dining room I call again. "Breakfast." I go to the kitchen, I fill the milk pan with water and let it soak. I pour my coffee, sit at the counter and eat my breakfast. I go upstairs to make your bed and clean your bathroom. I come down here to meet you and figure out what you want for lunch and dinner. And try to get you to think quickly so I can run to the market and get it bought before all the fresh stuff is bought up. Then, I start the day.

DRINKS BEFORE DINNER

BY E. L. DOCTOROW

Claudette and her husband throw a dinner party in their "modern, well-appointed" New York City apartment for their old and dear friend, a government secretary and Nobel Peace Prize winner. Before the guest of honor has arrived, another friend, Edgar, hijacks the conversation with a diatribe against the meaninglessness of their lives. When one guest sympathizes with Edgar's despair, claiming that even dead people in old movies, existing in an eternal state of high drama, have "more life" than she has, Claudette objects.

CLAUDETTE: Drama is to be avoided. I want to live my life as undramatically as possible. I want to live quietly and watch my children grow and keep my family fed and clean and enjoy beautiful things, and not be hurt by anyone. Besides which, whatever we know about our lives, we go on living them. Isn't that right? Even you, Andrea. Even Edgar. No matter what we say of it, life requires us to go on living it. It is the custom of life to go on with itself no matter what we say or what we feel. It has that aspect of requiring us to go on with it. Life is so totally careless of what we feel or what we know, or think we feel or think we know, that all our emotions and thoughts are continuously superseded by other emotions and other thoughts because life pushes on and forces us to continue living it. So that even if we are blissfully happy, it pushes on until we are not; even if we are in love, it pushes on until we are not; and even if we discover something marvelous or do something that makes us famous, it pushes on. It just goes through a whole lifetime of our feelings, careless of all of them, not giving a damn for any of them, except I suppose our last feeling before we die. When life stops to accommodate our feeling, we die. And what we said about it and felt about it is gone, and what we thought is gone, and our anger is gone, and the expression of our eyes and the character of our smiles, that's all gone. And if we knew how to embroider or sing "Bye Bye Blackbird," that's gone too.

TEENYTOWN

BY LAURIE CARLOS, JESSICA HAGEDORN, ROBBIE MCCAU

Although "Teenytown" is the title piece of this complex performance text, it stands alone, without direct reference to the rest of the play. In its original setting—an evening that mixed minstrel-show format with music, dance and multimedia visuals—the monologue was linked to the whole thematically as part of an exploration of racism in popular culture. The three performers staggered and alternated the lines randomly, in ethnic accents, as a comment on nontraditional casting. Someone using it as a solo, for auditions or an acting class, will need to come up with her own approach.

"Teenytown"

Once, there was a teeny tiny town ruled by a teeny tiny mayor . . . Teeny tiny goats roamed abandoned buildings and teeny tiny parking lots strewn with rubble and teeny tiny garbage. . . . Everyone was always hungry; you could see it in their tiny anxious faces and their teeny tiny eyes. (INCLUDING THE MAYOR!)

Teeny tiny boys and teeny tiny girls lived in teeny tiny mousetraps and ate cheese. . . . Five days a week, some of the more ambitious ones went to teeny tiny offices, smoked teeny tiny cigarettes, and slaved at part-time jobs where they never got to use their tiny minds. . . . No small matter. Two days a week, all the other teeny tiny boys and teeny tiny girls dreamed teeny tiny dreams which they diligently recorded on teeny tiny scraps of paper. A SLIGHT RIPPLE ON THE DIM HORIZON . . . A FAINT EXPLOSION FROM A DISTANCE . . . BUT A SHIT-STIRRER, NEVERTHELESS. To squelch rumors and prevent exotic and desirable aliens from ruining the neighborhood, the wily, teeny tiny mayor called town meetings on a monthly basis. Everyone was encouraged to complain at the same time, and when the noise died down, everyone always went away feeling much better.

At teeny tiny parties where no one was invited, teeny tiny poets compared dreams. They were always amazed at similarities in length and content; of course, it had been the same old teeny tiny town ever since anyone could remember—and they liked their dreams that way. . . . When the party was over (when the party was over), the teeny tiny poets fed their scraps to the ravenous, rabid goats who bleated, parked, and wailed in the squalid alleys outside holes they called "windows."

Days and nights passed in dissonant, familiar harmony—teeny tiny sunless days that turned without warning into terrifying moonless nights that seemed to go on forever. . . . The teeny tiny townsfolk took small comfort in promising each other that teeny tiny terrors could always be kept at bay. You know how the song goes: "You can be in my dream, if I can be in yours . . ."

WOMBmanWARs

BY JUDITH ALEXA JACKSON

Begun as a response to what the writer saw as the "'high-tech lynching' of Anita Hill" at the Clarence Thomas hearings and conceived as a solo performance, WOMBmanWARs *intercuts clips from that event with scenes from the Mike Tyson/Desiree Washington encounter, stylized movement theatre, domestic drama and standalone satirical monologues, like the first piece below. Jackson played the Gorilla with her back to the audience and a gorilla mask on the back of her head, but other actors in different contexts will find other ways.*

GORILLA: Was summa cum laude at Harvard. On the Dean's List at Yale. Taught law three years at Oxford. And was a Fulbright Fellow twice. My clothes are all designer. Elizabeth Arden does my nails. My face is by Borghese. My scent is politically correct. My hair was bought at Macy's. My wit is informed by the media. I avoid identifiable deviants; never socialize with liberals; and only speak Black English when it's absolutely necessary. While simultaneously cultivating a taste for arias by Mozart, I have successfully suppressed any urge to explore Hip Hop, Be Bop, or rap. I am amused by Afrocentricity, but invest enthusiastically in ethnic art. It is the least I can do for affirmative action. I subscribe to the *Wall Street Journal*, own stock in the *Washington Post*, and the *New York Times* is delivered on Saturdays to my rather large home in a treelined neighborhood that votes conservatively. What personal life I expose is created by my publicist. Granted I do not recognize myself on occasion. I do not know who I am. But surely you must see me. My mirror reflects the American dream. I am America the beautiful. Believe me. No *Gorilla* could have achieved all of this. So why do I get the impression that your perception of me has still not changed?

(Mannerisms become increasingly apelike) You sittin' there staring at me like you've just seen a walkin', talkin' ape. Some kind of an overgrown jungle bunny in a monkey suit. Do I have my head on backwards? I graduated summa cum laude. OK? So I ain't tryin' to hear dat see. Homey don't play dat. *(Gets up and begins to move downstage menacingly)* I don't want to have to go dere. What are you looking at? What does it take for you to see me. Don't let me have to go dere. Don't let me have to act like no nigger! I ain't tryin' to play dat see.

4

"WHY DON'T YOU TALK TO A PSYCHIATRIST?"

RECKLESS

BY CRAIG LUCAS

Rachel runs away from home one Christmas Eve, changes her name and embarks on a new life. Here, in her first meeting with a psychiatrist, she tries to explain what happened.

RACHEL: Well, last Christmas? Christmas Eve? My husband Tom is all tucked into bed like a little kid and our two boys are in their beds, I've just tucked them in, and I tell Tom how perfect it all seems, I've never been so happy, which is true. And . . . Well, my father was allergic to dogs, you know, and Tom didn't like puppies, so I never said anything about wanting a puppy, but I was thinking about it. And I was looking out into the snow and talking about Alaska or something, but I was thinking about how people in books and movies are always getting puppies on Christmas and you never see anybody having to clean up the □□□ or get hit by cars. You always see them with a big red bow and the kids are smiling and—but I didn't say anything, I was just thinking it. I didn't want Tom to feel guilty if he hadn't gotten me a puppy which I knew he hadn't because he hates them, so it was just a private little something I was thinking about and that's all I needed really was to think about it and rub its little imaginary ears. And we were watching the news, I remember, and suddenly I realize Tom's upset. So naturally I assume he knows I really want a puppy, so I go to comfort him, because I don't care about it, really, if it's going to make him unhappy, I don't even mention it, I just give him a big hug and tell him it's Christmas and be happy and he says he's taken a contract out on my life. Maybe I'm overreacting. Or he's kidding, which I think he must be. But anyway, I wind up spending Christmas with this man I meet at the Arco station and his girlfriend who is crippled and deaf, she says, you know, with hand signals until suddenly she just turns to me and starts saying how she had to pretend she was deaf to get the attention of this man we're all living with who's changed his name and run away and she's changed her name and I've changed my name and we're all working in the same place and she's telling me all these secrets and all of a sudden she says, "Why don't you talk to a psychiatrist?"

TALK RADIO

BY ERIC BOGOSIAN

"Nighttalk" with Barry Champlain on a Cleveland, Ohio, talk-radio station attracts callers the host considers "yellow-bellied, spineless, bigoted, quivering, drunken, insomniatic, paranoid, disgusting, perverted, voyeuristic little obscene phone callers." Denise is one.

DENISE: I'm scared, Barry. □□□ you know, like we've got a garbage disposal in our sink in the kitchen, I mean my mother's kitchen. □□□ and sometimes a teaspoon will fall into the garbage disposal. □□□ ya, so like, you know how you feel when you have to reach down into that garbage disposal and you have to feel around down there for that teaspoon. You don't want to do it. Who knows what's down there? Could be garbage, a piece of something, so much stuff goes down there . . . or germs, which you can't see. You can't see germs, but if they're gonna be anywhere, they're gonna be down that disposal. They grow there, see? They come back up the pipes. Salmonella, yeast, cancer, even the common cold, who knows? But, Barry, even without all that, what if, and I'm just saying "what if," 'cause it would probably never happen, but what if the garbage disposal came on while your hand is down there? □□□ I get so scared of thinking about it that I usually leave the teaspoon there. I don't even try to get it out. But then I'm afraid that my mother will get mad if she finds it down there, so I turn the disposal on, trying to make it go down the drain. But all it does is make a huge racket. And I stand in the middle of the kitchen and the spoon goes around and around and I get sort of paralyzed, you know? It makes a lot of noise, incredible noise. But Barry, I kind of like that noise, because I know the teaspoon is getting destroyed and annihilated and that's good 'cause I hate the teaspoon for scaring me like that. □□□ Well it's not just the disposal, it's everything. What about insects? Termites. Hornets. Spiders. Ants. Centipedes. Mites. You can't even see the mites, they're like the germs. Tiny, impossible to see! I like things to be clean, you know. Dirty ashtrays bother me. ☐☐☐ The mailman brings me unsolicited mail and the postage stamp was licked by someone with AIDS. Right? My mother is a threat to my life by persisting in going out there. ☐☐☐ Do you know that there's this dust storm in California that has these little fungus spores in it? And these spores get in people's lungs and it goes into their bloodstreams and grows inside them and kills them? Strange air . . . strange air . . . you have to . . . Oh! There's my mother. I hear her key in the door. She'll kill me if she finds out I used the phone.

RAISED IN CAPTIVITY

BY NICKY SILVER

When her last patient terminated therapy, Dr. Hillary MacMahon blamed herself. Convinced that the patient's abandonment was proof of her own innate badness, the no-longer-practicing psychologist stabbed herself in the hand, threw her TV in the river, clothed herself in rags and generally opted for self-mutilation as the path to sanctity. She explains to the audience.

HILLARY: AS I WAS SAYING!!! ☐☐☐ I had no God. And although, intellectually, I have always found the idea of God, per se, rather far-fetched and revoltingly patriarchal, and *organized* religion seems, to me, to be little more than another systematic mechanism by which the plutocratic echelon controls the educational and economic underclass, it does also, obviously, provide that subclass a system with which those who feel burdened by sociologically imposed guilt can purge those feelings and continue their lives in a clean, new, virgin state.

I went to the church near my house and told the priest that I was bad and I wanted to make a confession. I said, "Father, I am bad. I am pocked with the mark of Cain." He asked me when I last made a confession, and I told him never. He said he was unclear as to what, exactly, my sins were. And I told him that I couldn't be any clearer right now, but that my spirit was spent from shouldering a tremendous, nameless guilt. Then he asked me if I wanted to buy a chance in the church raffle. The grand prize was a microwave. I told him no. I wouldn't feel comfortable buying a raffle and supporting an organization that refuses to recognize women as priests. I couldn't contribute because I believe a woman has the right to control her own body. I feel condoms should be distributed in the public schools because of the AIDS plague, and I don't think everyone who uses birth control pills goes to hell. He told me to get out and return only after I'd rethought my positions. Apparently the price of absolution is the sacrifice of one's own moral code. So I left without redemption and it is up to me to create my penance. I wear these rags as a crown of thorns. I hate them. I have plenty of money. My father invested wisely and left me a chain of motor lodges when he died, but I've been wearing the same dress for five months now. I smell miserable, but I still feel guilty. I tried to give up television—I thought that would be sufficiently torturous to leave me feeling clean and reborn. So I threw my set into the river. But I found myself browsing, decadently, for hours, in appliance stores. I am wretchedness itself. That is why I have decided to put my eyes out with this screwdriver. Excuse me. *(She turns her back to the audience and raises the screwdriver high over her head)* I WILL BE CLEAN!!!

FAT MEN IN SKIRTS

BY NICKY SILVER

Popo greets the audience from the hospital where she is about to meet and fall in love with a man who has spent many years as a cannibal and, more recently, murdered both his parents. She is a "very cheery mental patient."

POPO: I am Popo Martin. My friends call me Popo Martin. Dr. Nestor says I'm a paranoid schizophrenic. I think I have Marnie's disease.

You know, like Tippi Hedren in that movie. When I see red, I mean, I have an episode. Although sometimes it happe don't see red. And sometimes I see red and it doesn't happen. . . the most popular girl in the hospital. I gets lots of visitors! I was a cheerleader. I'd do a cheer for you now, but I don't have my pom-poms. All my teachers love me. The girls on the squad come to visit me every Sunday. The principal sent me a get-well note and the boys autographed a football. You can ask anyone in school about me, and they'd all say the same thing. Popo Martin is always cheerful. Popo Martin is a natural leader. Popo Martin looks on the bright side. Popo Martin has a smile on her lips and a kind word for a saddened stranger. Which is probably why everyone was so surprised when it happened. I tried to kill myself! I took thirty-five sleeping pills out of my mother's purse. I didn't want to smile anymore. My jaw hurts. And whistling gives me a headache. I want, more than anything, to wallow in a hopeless depression—but it just goes against my grain. So I tried to kill myself. That's why I'm here.

THE VAMPIRES

BY HARRY KONDOLEON

Cc's husband, Ian, has been acting strangely. He's a theatre critic whose recent reviews publicly humiliated his brother and pushed an actor to suicide. Cc and Ian have just returned from an awards ceremony at which they both made spectacles of themselves—he for heckling a winner and she for wearing a grotesque dress of her own design. This monologue jump-starts the play and ends when Ian runs into the room from upstairs, bites Cc's neck and sucks her blood.

cc: You have got to show me some consideration. Do you hear me? I thought you wanted to go to this ceremony. I didn't want to go. I thought it meant something to you. I broke my neck trying to finish this dress for tonight. You make fun of it in front of the first group of people we meet—how am I supposed to interpret something like that, Ian? Am I supposed to take it as a joke? How can I? Come down here! Oh who am I kidding with this dress anyway?! □□□ The invitation says black tie and half the people show up in dungarees and pullovers so I look like a Mardi Gras float and then the editor of that coarse magazine you used to work for points out the pins in my dress as if she were uncovering a sex scandal! Ian! Ian! Are you coming down here? I'm trying to be understanding, Ian. I know you're going through a difficult career-transition period. Maybe some of your behavior these last few weeks has something to do with that actor's tragedy. That's not your fault, Ian, many actors get bad reviews, they just have to live with it, no one's to blame, you were just doing your job. But when you started laughing tonight during that woman's acceptance speech I was never so embarrassed in my entire life and you being one of the judges! But then I've lost count of most of the humiliations: you mimicking people at checkout counters, alienating each and every person we meet, contradicting me in front of my friends. I know I have very idealistic ideas about love but this marriage, Ian, is hitting some uncharted new low.

THE VAMPIRES

BY HARRY KONDOLEON

Things are going badly for Pat, too. Pat's daughter Zivia has run away from home and is probably shooting up drugs; her husband, Ed, a carpenter, is obsessed with a play he's written "about the colonists, the Indians, the revolution, the whole scene . . . projected and juxtaposed—whatever—upon or with today's problems." Pat's come looking for the thirteen-year-old Zivia at the home of her sister-in-law, Cc, who has just been bitten and bloodsucked by her own husband, a wanna-be vampire. Not one to allow herself to cry, Pat is, Kondoleon writes, "agitated."

PAT: I know I should have called. I'm so worried and upset I couldn't sleep so I got in the car and just drove. Is Zivia here with you? You can tell me, C. There's no use hiding it. I won't be jealous. I know you two are very close and Zivia's very fond of you and all so I wouldn't be surprised. In fact, you're the first person I thought of. I thought, Zivia's gone to visit her Aunt C, that's all. Is she here? No? C, you know I can't take this, this kind of extreme worry. I mean since Axel four years ago my nerves have been shot to hell. So I can't be accused of jumping to conclusions when Zivia doesn't come home Friday and all day Saturday! I mean, what is going on?! I'm not an overprotective mother, far from it. Perhaps I should be. Maybe that's where I've gone wrong but you don't have any children, C, so you can't sit there and accuse me! I mean it's one thing to go off on a day of shopping with a niece and quite another to raise a daughter all year every year worrying what's going to happen to her. So don't accuse me of anything! Do you know that two girls in Zivia's class took their own lives—two! In my class there were none. Maybe it's nowadays the rage but, frankly, I'm terrified! You know what kind of touchy type Zivia is and you know my pop took a shot at himself. I mean that kind of thing is maybe hereditary. I don't know. I just don't want to set anything off and you know what Ed's like. He found some pot or something in her room and started yelling and cursing at the top of his lungs. I mean pot's no big deal, C. All the kids smoke pot. I smoked pot. Big deal, I said, Ed, calm down! Does my hair look funny? It didn't curl the way they said it would on the box. So she's not here?

5

"MY FIRST MASTERPIECE"

PAINTING CHURCHES

BY TINA HOWE

Mags, a young artist on the verge of her first worldly success, returns to the Boston home of her aging parents. An eccentric old couple of pure WASP stock, they have forgotten, or tried to forget, the story she reminds them of: "my first masterpiece." The story began when she was banished from the dinner table to her room for swirling colorful patterns on her plate with food squished through her front teeth. Her unappetizing behavior was the result of mealtime tensions and proprieties that made it impossible for her to swallow a bite. The result of her six-month bedroom exile—with dinners on trays—was her first work of art.

MAGS: It was wintertime, because I noticed I'd left some crayons on top of my radiator and they'd melted down into these beautiful shimmering globs, like spilled jello, trembling and pulsing. □□□ Naturally, I wanted to try it myself, so I grabbed a red one and pressed it down against the hissing lid. It oozed and bubbled like raspberry jam! □□□ I mean, that radiator was really hot! It took incredible will power not to let go, but I held on, whispering, "Mags, if you let go of this crayon, you'll be run over by a truck on Newberry Street, so help you God!" . . . So I pressed down harder, my fingers steaming and blistering. □□□ Once I'd melted one, I was hooked! I finished off my entire supply in one night, mixing color over color until my head swam! . . . The heat, the smell, the brilliance that sank and rose . . . I'd never felt such exhilaration! . . . Every week I spent my allowance on crayons. I must have cleared out every box of Crayolas in the city! □□□ AFTER THREE MONTHS THAT RADIATOR WAS . . . SPECTACULAR! I MEAN, IT LOOKED LIKE SOME COLOSSAL FRUITCAKE, FIVE FEET TALL . . . ! □□□ It was a knockout; shimmering with pinks and blues, lavenders and maroons, turquoise and golds, oranges and creams. . . . For every color, I imagined a taste . . . YELLOW: lemon curls dipped in sugar . . . RED: glazed cherries laced with rum . . .

GREEN: tiny peppermint leaves veined with chocolate . . . PURPLE:—
□□□ And then the frosting . . . ahhhh, the frosting! A satiny mix of
white and silver . . . I kept it hidden under blankets during the day. . . .
My huge . . . *(She starts laughing)* looming . . . teetering sweet—
□□□ I was so . . . *hungry.* . . losing weight every week. I looked like
a scarecrow what with the bags under my eyes and bits of crayon
wrapper leaking out of my clothes. It's a wonder you didn't notice.
But finally you came to my rescue . . . if you could call what happened
a rescue. It was more like a rout! □□□ The winter was almost over. . . .
It was very late at night. . . . I must have been having a nightmare
because suddenly you and Daddy were at my bed, shaking me. . . .
I quickly glanced towards the radiator to see if it was covered. . . . *It
wasn't!* It glittered and towered in the moonlight like some . . . gigan-
tic Viennese pastry! You followed my gaze and saw it. Mummy
screamed . . . "WHAT HAVE YOU GOT IN HERE? . . . MAGS, WHAT
HAVE YOU BEEN DOING?" . . . She crept forward and touched it, and
then jumped back. "IT'S FOOD!" she cried. . . "IT'S ALL THE FOOD
SHE'S BEEN SPITTING OUT! OH, GARDNER, IT'S A MOUNTAIN OF
ROTTING GARBAGE!" □□□ Of course in a sense you were right. It
was a monument of my castoff dinners, only I hadn't built it with
food. . . . I found my own materials. I was languishing with hunger,
but oh, dear Mother . . . I FOUND MY OWN MATERIALS . . . !

LIVE AND IN COLOR!

BY DANITRA VANCE

*In the epilogue to her one-woman show, Danitra Vance appeared in
bed with* The Complete Works of Shakespeare. *Just as she had transformed into numerous other characters throughout this evening of,
mostly, extended monologues, here the versatile African-American
performer became Flotilda Williams (as Juliet).*

FLOTILDA: I'm Flotilda Williams. I'm a classical actress. Right now I am
in a production downtown with a group called Shakespeare in the
Slums. We are doing a play by Mister William Shakespeares call

Romeo and Juliet. And me, I'm Juliet, okay. Now what I want to do for y'all is to extrapolate and explainate on what be going on in the show. The show starts and a lot of things happen but really we just gonna skip all that and get to the good part, where I come in.

I'm at this party, a lot of fancy people there and I'm there and I'm there with my Mama and the Nurse. Even so I manage to meet this guy. A very good-lookin' guy, makes me laugh with his funny funny jokes, probably got some money. So I like him. His name is Romeo. I have thus extrapolated the title—Romeo and me, Juliet, okay.

Anyway the party is not even half over when my Mama and the Nurse say, "Juliet it's time to go." And I say, "Okay, I'll be right with you." So she find Romeo and they say goodbye by touching finger-tips like this, *(Gesture)* completely missing the point.

After that I go home and I'm trying to be asleep but I can't sleep 'cause I'm thinkin' 'bout this guy. How much I want to see him again. How much I want to talk to him again. How much I want to do things with him I've never done before.

Now in the meantime the guy, Romeo, is down in the alleyway lookin' up in my window. Now he not lookin' up in my window because he a freak or nothin' like that, he lookin' up in my window because he like me, okay. Then he start to talk to hisself. Now, he not talkin' to hisself 'cause he crazy or nothin', he talk to hisself 'cause it's a play, okay. People in plays talk to theyselves a lot.

And he say, he say,

"But soft! what light throo yonder windo' break?"

That's when I break through the window.

BUCK

BY RONALD RIBMAN

Shirley plays the sluttish victim in a murder-reenactment show on a sleazy cable station. The reenactments—sheer sex, violence and action—are only a notch above porno shorts cranked out for peep shows. Shirley, though, who hasn't hesitated to sleep with "pigs" to get as far as she's gotten, aspires to more. She believes that Buck

Halloran, her producer, might understand and encourage her dreams.

SHIRLEY: Mr. Halloran, could I ask you something? □□□ Do you think I could be an actress? I mean if I went to one of those acting classes and had lessons and really worked at it? Or do you think I'm just fooling myself? You see I've put aside a little money over the years and I wouldn't mind spending it if I thought I had a chance of really becoming a good actress. But if I was just fooling myself . . . it wouldn't be just losing the money . . . you know what I mean? □□□ Because that's what I really want, you know? I've been thinking about it for a long time, ever since I was stripping down in Dallas. □□□ Well, what it was was that I was always trying to put some words in my act . . . nothing set, or anything like that . . . just what came into my mind. I'd come out and say . . . *(Getting to her knees, snapping her fingers and in an instant creating her character: a shimmying, breast-jiggling stripper)* "Hi. My name is Francine. What's yours?" *(Stopping her motion and turning to Buck)* That's the name I was using down in Texas. I changed it to Babette in Oklahoma because it sounded more French. And they'd say, "Frank," or "John," or whatever. And then I'd say . . . *(Getting up on her knees again and going through the same routine)* "I need a bodyguard. Would you like to be my bodyguard?" *(Sitting back down again)* You see my full stage name was Francine the Body, so there was a double meaning for the words. I also had a routine I did with a rose. That was when I was supposed to be the Rose of Sharon. You see I had a lot of parts I made up for myself: Babette the French maid . . . the Devil's Angel . . . *(Placing a finger on her hip and making a sound suggestive of heat)* tsss! Very hot! Marie Antoinette . . . *(Drawing her finger across her throat)* Sinderella. *Sin*derella, with an S. . . . When I was Sinderella I showed the whole transformation using little hand puppets like mice to take off my clothes . . . *(Getting to her knees again, making little "eek, eek" sounds as she pretends her fingers are mice pulling at her clothing. Finishing, she sits down again)* But my favorite was the Rose of Sharon. When I was the Rose of Sharon all the decorations on the stage were like petals, and I pinned a rose to the front of my G-string, and then I would lift my skirt and ask if anyone would like to pluck my rose. And someone would always say he would, and try to reach out and grab the rose, but I would never let him. I did it all by myself. *(Lying down on the stage and simulating the action she describes)*

I laid down on the stage and I plucked all the petals of my rose and blew them away. *(Sitting up again)* The manager thought it was a good idea because the boys like to say things to you while you're working, and it works out great if you can give them little bits of prop to keep or say things back. Most of the girls just made noises . . . little kissy sounds or things like that . . . but I was the first one there to actually use words, or tell a story.

6

"THINGS YOU KIDS DON'T KNOW"

THE WASH

BY PHILIP KAN GOTANDA

Masi, a Japanese-American woman sixty-seven years old, has left Nobu, her husband of four decades, and moved by herself into a small apartment. She continues, though, to do his wash, stopping by their family home each week to pick up dirty clothes and drop off clean ones. Gradually, Masi develops a life of her own, including a relationship with another man, a widower, Sadao. In this scene, Masi has just informed her two grown daughters that she plans to tell Nobu that she wants a divorce in order to marry again.

MASI: Dad was always trying to beat me down, every little thing. "How come you can't do this, how come you can't do that"—nothing was ever right. Every time I opened my mouth I was always wrong—he was always right. He always had to be right. *(Pause)* There are things you kids don't know. I didn't want to talk about them to you, but . . . Daddy and I, we didn't sleep □□□ together. Every time I wanted to, he would push me away. Ten, fifteen years he didn't want me. *(Pause)* We were having one of our arguments, just like always. And he was going on and on about how it was my fault this and my fault that. And I was trying to explain my side of it, when he turned on me, "Shut up, Mama. You don't know anything. You're *stupid*." Stupid. After forty-two years of letting him be right he called me that. And I understood. He didn't even need me to make him be right anymore. He just needed me to be stupid. I was tired. I couldn't fight him anymore. He won. He finally made me feel like shit. □□□ That was the night I left him and came over to your place. □□□ I like Sadao. I like Sadao very much.

PAINTING CHURCHES

BY TINA HOWE

Mags, a painter, has just accused her mother of treating her father "like a child or some dimwitted serving boy." Fanny fires back as her husband, Gardner, an eminent poet who in his seventies has grown forgetful, dotty and incontinent, sits on the floor amid a lifetime of books and papers and makes a paper airplane.

FANNY: What is he to *you?*. . . I mean, what do you give him from yourself that costs you something? . . . Hmmmmmm? . . . *(Imitating Mags)* "Oh, hi Daddy, it's great to see you again. How have you been? . . . Gee, I love your hair. It's gotten so . . . *white!*" . . . What color do you expect it to get when he's this age? . . . I mean, if you care so much how he looks, why don't you come and see him once in a while? . . . But oh, no . . . you have your paintings to do and your shows to put on. You just come and see us when the whim strikes. *(Imitating Mags)* "Hey, you know what would be really great? . . . To do a portrait of you! I've always wanted to paint you, you're such great subjects!". . . *Paint* us?! . . . What about opening your eyes and really *seeing* us? . . . Noticing what's going on around here for a change! It's all over for Daddy and me. This is it! "Finita la commedia!" . . . All I'm trying to do is exit with a little flourish; have some fun. . . . What's so terrible about that? . . . It can get pretty grim around here, in case you haven't noticed . . . Daddy, tap-tap-tapping out his nonsense all day; me traipsing around to the thrift shops trying to amuse myself. . . . He never keeps me company anymore; never takes me out anywhere. . . . I'd put a bullet through my head in a minute, but then who'd look after him? . . . What do you think we're moving to the cottage for? . . . So I can watch him like a hawk and make sure he doesn't get lost. Do you think that's anything to look forward to?. . . Being Daddy's nursemaid out in the middle of nowhere? I'd much rather stay here in Boston with the few friends I have left, but you can't always do what you want in this world! "L'homme propose, Dieu dispose!" . . . If you want to paint us so badly, you ought to paint us as we really are. There's your picture!

WOMBmanWARs

BY JUDITH ALEXA JACKSON

The story of an African-American couple, Sapphire and Danny, and their daughter, Danisha, runs through this solo performance piece that, elsewhere, combines documentary-theatre devices with stylized movement and political satire. The following scene ends WOMBman-WARs, as Sapphire visits her sleeping daughter's room. (Danisha is her only daughter; an earlier pregnancy ended in miscarriage.) The monologue's themes are the play's as well: the choosing of the male over the female and the wars women have—even inside them-selves—as they try to be whole in the world. These issues also occupy the conflicted center of Sapphire's life.

SAPPHIRE *(Peeping into Danisha's room)*: Danisha? Are you awake. *(She enters and sits on edge of bed)* I guess it's just as well you are asleep. I don't think I came in here to talk to you as much as myself. Today is the last day.

Couldn't sleep. I was up watching *Sophie's Choice*. Didn't pay too much attention 'til one of the Nazis asked Sophie to choose which one of her children should live. The boy or the girl.

I saw Sophie standing there, holding both of her children close . . . trying to choose who would be cremated. How could she choose? How could any mother choose? I saw her mind working. He might be a warrior. He might change the world. It was a man's world to change. I knew her choice before she ever opened her mouth. I would have made the same choice. Death for the girl.

And that's when it hit me Danisha. I have never chosen you. I have never chosen life for you.

Today is the last day. When you were born, and they told me you were a girl, I was so unhappy I actually cried.

My heart knew it would be my job to break you. To break your spirit before you were grown and some stranger came along and did it. I had to do to you what my mother did to me and her mother to her. To protect you from your dreams.

But no more, my darling precious daughter. I don't know how. I don't even know why. I only know today is the last day. The last day. The last day I stand back and watch your spirit cry. *(She tucks cov-*

ers around Danisha) I choose you. I choose you. *(She hugs Danisha and rocks with her gently)*

STILL LIFE

BY EMILY MANN

Having lived through a brutal, alcoholic marriage, Nadine is now intensely involved with Mark, a married ex-Marine who shares with her (but never takes out on her) the violence he experienced and committed in Vietnam. She is more than a decade older than Mark, and, like him, she is an artist. She speaks directly to the audience, as if to an interviewer, in this testimonial-style play. When she talks about her husband, she is referring to her ex-husband.

NADINE:
Oh, God.
I'm worried about us.
I keep this quiet little knowledge with me every day.
I don't tell my husband about it
I don't tell my kids,
or Mark.
Or anyone.
But something has fallen apart.
I'm having trouble being a mother.
How can you believe in sending your children to special classes
when you know it doesn't matter?
Oh,
I worry, I worry,
I worry one of my daughters
will be walking down the street
and get raped or mugged by someone who is angry or hungry.
I worry I have these three beautiful daughters (pieces of life)
who I have devoted my whole life to,
who I've put all my energy into—bringing up—raising—
and then somebody up there goes crazy one day

and pushes the "go" button and
phew! bang, finished, the end.
I worry that my daughters won't want to give birth
because of my bad birthing experience.
And I worry that they *will* want to give birth.

I worry that—
Well, one of my daughters does blame me
for the divorce
because I have protected them from knowing
what kind of man their father really is.

(I worry that I worry too much about all this
and I worry that I really don't worry enough about it all.)
I worry so much it makes me sick.
I work eighteen hours a day just to pay the bills.
This year, I work on the feminist caucus,
I do my portraits, run my magazine, organize civic events.
I hold two jobs and more.
I invited my dear, sweet, ninety-one-year-old uncle
to come die at my house.

I go to recitals, shopping, graduation,
I don't go through the ritual
of getting undressed at night.
I sleep with my shoes on.
My husband's alcoholism has ruined us.
(Forty-five thousand dollars in debt.)

I don't dare get angry anymore.
Can you imagine what would happen,
if I got angry?
My children . . .

(Can't go on.)

DON'T YOU EVER CALL ME ANYTHING BUT MOTHER

BY JOHN O'KEEFE

This monologue is taken from a play-length monologue. Doris rambles from room to room, drinking and drunken, chain-smoking and talking to her son, John E, whom we never see (he has left her). A bony, toothless woman in her sixties, she has just emerged from the bathroom, from which a harsh light reveals her painted with powder, covered with bright rouge, smeared with lipstick and made-up with false lashes and eye shadow ringing what look like black eyes.

DORIS: Hello, John E, this is your mother. Do you like me? I can still draw an eye or two. Do you remember what I looked like with those shoulder pads and the Scottish plaid? I'm Irish, you know, but I look good in things like that with my hair all piled up like on a Coca-Cola sign out of the forties. I had slim legs and a lithe body and champagne breasts and my skin was creamy white with warm little freckles on it. John E, look at me. I'm going to tell you something you should know about. Look at this body. Do you know what this body is for? It is for the lust of God to have his way with me. All . . . the . . . way, John all the way. To plant a baby inside of me. To plant a baby inside of me. That's where you were. You were up inside of me. *(She cups her hands between her legs)* Up here. Haven't I ever told you about that stuff? Let me tell you, my darling son. A man, John E, a man put his thing in me. And it made him feel terribly good. That thing, that big thing of his. It made him want to come. Do you know what "want to come" means? It means that he can't stand the pleasure of it so much that he dies in me. He dies in me. He dies in me, John E, and when he does his whole body gets hard and starts to shudder and he starts pumping and pumping and he makes these strange cries like a baby wanting his mother and his face gets red like a poor sweet thing and he begins to weep and then, John E, then he comes. *(Mysteriously)* He comes inside of my body and I hold him and I say, "Yes, yes, my sweet darling," and I rock him and caress him and he gets all soft and cuddly and he just curls up and goes to sleep. But I don't sleep, John E, no, I don't sleep. I lie there in the dark and feel his cum go sticky, feel it up inside of me, sending its magic into me, red and wanting and hurting for the magic that will wear your eyes and dress in your skin. *(She smiles knowingly, almost winking)* Someday you'll come, John E. You'll know when you come. You'll know it for sure.

THE FOOD CHAIN

BY NICKY SILVER

Amanda Dolor has been married for three weeks to a man she met a week before. Her husband, Ford, a filmmaker, has been missing for two of those weeks. Finally, in the middle of one night, she dials a crisis hotline, switches to speakerphone and tells her story—the monologues below are two parts of it—to the woman on the other end. Silver describes Amanda as an attractive, highly verbal and high-strung intellectual in her early thirties. She's a poet and very thin.

AMANDA: Yes. We're back in the city. It's Monday morning. We had breakfast. And after breakfast, he told me that he wanted to go for a walk. So naturally, I started to put my shoes on. I thought he meant together.—But he said, he wanted to go alone. He was working on an idea for a film, mapping it out in his mind, as it were. I was a little hurt, to be honest. But I understand that the creative process is a very delicate dance. Ford is a genius. I'd seen all of his films before we'd ever even met, and I always found them—searing. Just searing and penetrating in a very powerful way. So, I didn't want to question his process. It's very important that an artist be nurtured. . . . So he went out. And I took a shower. This was about noon. After that, I tried to do some writing. I'm a poet—vocationally. That's what I do. I was working on a new poem: "Untitled 103," and I was very absorbed in the poem. It's about wind. Wind as a metaphor for God as a force in our lives. Or the lack thereof. The stillness, the arbitrariness of a random world. And the work was going very well. I was really just vomiting images like spoiled sushi (that may be an ill-considered metaphor but you get my gist). I was absorbed and productive.

I'd written—three lines, I think, when I looked at the clock and it was ten-thirty. This happens sometimes, when I'm writing. It's as if I fall into a hole in the time-space continuum. I am pulled—I've strayed.

So it's ten-thirty and I haven't heard from Ford. But I didn't worry.

I was unfamiliar with his process and it seemed possible that he'd been out walking for *ten and a half hours*.

So I tried to go to sleep. But I couldn't sleep! I tossed and turned. I had visions in my head of Ford in a hospital, or dead in a ditch, the victim of wandering thugs. And then, of course, I started thinking . . . nothing happened to him! He hates me. He's gone. We rushed into this and now he's left me. It's over. I did something wrong. I was too aggressive! Or too passive! Or too passive-aggressive! I went into a shame spiral! And I cried, and I cursed and I prayed to God that this was a terrible dream, and that any minute I'd wake up and Ford'd be lying next to me!

And then the phone rang—thank God! I looked at the clock: six-fifteen. It was Ford! I was so relieved! "Ford! WHERE ARE YOU!?"—I tried to keep the panic out of my voice. I didn't want to seem, for a minute, the overbearing wife. He said he was fine. "I just need some time," he said. "I'm working on a film and I need some time."........And then, he hung up. He hung up. And haven't heard from him since.

THE FOOD CHAIN

BY NICKY SILVER

Another note: the later lines here refer to Amanda's first passionate night of lovemaking with Ford, after which she'd realized that the neighbors she'd sometimes watched through her apartment windows, and whose isolation filled her with "a huge sorrow . . . a mammoth despair," could see them have sex.

AMANDA: Well, I left my apartment. It was about noon and it was a nice day, so I thought I'd walk to her [my friend Binky's] house. She lives on 75th and Columbus, which, I realize, is a very long walk, but I thought the exercise would do me good—I hadn't eaten anything yet, so I stopped at the diner on my corner, for some breakfast, and I picked up a newspaper so I'd have something to do.

I was reading my paper when the waiter came over and asked if I was . . . *alone*. Well! It was obvious that I was *alone*! I was sitting

there, in a booth, by myself—did he think I thought I had
nary friend with me?! I was *alone*! Did he have to rub it in
trying to be funny? Did he think he was, in some way, be
me? It was in his tone. He said, "Are you alone?" But what I
to say was, "You're alone. *Aren't you!?*"—And I can't imagine that
he's not alone every single day of his miserable, *pathetic* life! He has
terrible skin. And it's not attractive. Not the way bad skin, or at least
the remnants of bad skin, is attractive on some people. On some
men!! It's never attractive on women—have you noticed that? Just
one more example of the injustices we are forced to suffer! If we
have bad skin, we're grotesque! Let a man have bad skin and he can
be Richard Burton for God's sake! I HATE BEING A WOMAN!!

I've strayed.

The point is this waiter has terrible skin, and greasy hair and his
breath stinks of something dead and his face is entirely too close to
mine, and he insults me with his breath and his tone of voice and
asks if I'm alone. I feel my face go flush and I want to rip his head
off! I'd *like* to pull his hair out, only I'd never be able to get a decent
grip—it looks as if it hasn't been washed in a decade! I want to pick
up my butter knife and stab in his sunken, caved-in chest! But! I simply respond, *(Grandly)* "No, I'm married, thank you."

(Pause) I realize, now, of course, that my answer was illogical. I
realize that it was inappropriate. But, at the time, it was all I could
think to say.

Well, he leans back and, really, in the most supercilious manner,
he leers at me and intones, "I meant, are you *eating* alone." "I KNEW
WHAT YOU MEANT!" I KNEW WHAT HE MEANT! I don't know why I
said what I said, I just said it! He made me sick. I hope he dies. I
shouted, "I KNEW WHAT YOU MEANT!" And I am not a person who
shouts, generally. I don't like shouting. It hurts to shout and it hurts
to be shouted at. My mother shouted quite a bit and I always thought
the veins in her neck looked like the roots of a tree. But I shouted.
Everyone looked at me . . . because I was standing. I didn't mean to
be standing. I didn't remember standing, but I was. I was standing. I
must've leapt up when I shouted. So I was standing and everyone
was staring at me. The place was very crowded, much more crowded than I ever recall seeing it before. And suddenly, it occurred to me,
that these *people, my neighbors*, gawking at me in endless silence,
were the very same people who had watched Ford and myself have
sex that first night when we met. I was humiliated! I thought I would

die! Or be sick! I was certain I was going to be sick right there at my table, standing up, being stared at! And then everyone in the neighborhood would mutter under their breath, every time they saw me, "Oh there goes that woman. We've seen her have sex, and we've seen her vomit."

I WOULD LIKE, AT SOME POINT IN MY LIFE, TO CLING, WITH WHATEVER ENERGY I HAVE, TO MY DIGNITY!

GETTING OVER TOM

BY LENORA CHAMPAGNE

Taken from a longer, solo performance—what the author calls a "high energy" "talking dance"—this piece recounts an evening spent in Montreal. The speaker recalls having traveled there to celebrate Christmas with her friend Patricia, whose husband, Gabriel, had recently walked out on her. Throughout the visit, the speaker struggled to resolve anxiety and indecision about her own lover, Tom: Should she leave him? Was he right when he accused her of needing to keep control? What is she waiting for? There is no other mention or description of Claude, who in the excerpt below asks the speaker to dance.

That evening
Patricia and I
talked about her marriage
and I remembered the wedding
where all these French Canadians
were doing this amazing dance
and I was so moved
and felt ashamed.
I thought,
"These are my people.
But I've forgotten this dance."
Then Claude came up to me and said
"Do you want to dance?"

I guess he could tell I did
since I'd taken my shoes off.
And I said
"Yes."
I was afraid
because I'd never learned
how to follow.
When the spinning began
he said
"Look into my eyes."
"You must look into my eyes."
And I realized
"I have to!
Or else,
I'll fall!"

It was disturbing
at first
to look into his eyes.
I felt exposed, vulnerable,
without polite distance
as protection.
For a while
I thought
what was scary
was letting go
of self-control
and placing trust in another—
a man—
to keep from falling.
Then I realized it wasn't about
placing trust
in another—
although it was about
letting go—
but about
balance.
When you're spinning
while you're holding someone
the center can't be

in each dancer
or in one
or the other.
It has to be
somewhere
in the space
between the two.

So, after learning this,
I was distresed
when Gabriel
walked out
Patricia's door.
Then Patricia said
she had to bake some cakes
for a christening the next day
so I went to bed early
even though it was
Christmas Eve.

COMPANY

BY STEPHEN SONDHEIM AND GEORGE FURTH

*A date that will end in bed: April, a flight attendant who describes her-
self as "very dumb," visits Robert's bachelor pad for the first time.
As he seduces her, she speaks.*

APRIL: Right after I became an airline stewardess, a friend of mine
who had a garden apartment gave me a cocoon for my bedroom. He
collects things like that, insects and caterpillars and all that . . . It was
attached to a twig and he said one morning I'd wake up to a beautiful butterfly in my bedroom—when it hatched. He told me that
when they come out they're soaking wet and there is a drop of blood
there, too—isn't that fascinating—but within an hour they dry off
and then they begin to fly. Well, I told him I had a cat. I had a cat then,

but he said just put the cocoon somewhere where the cat couldn't get at it . . . which is impossible, but what can you do? So I put it up high on a ledge where the cat never went, and the next morning it was still there, at least so it seemed safe to leave it. Well, anyway, almost a week later very, very early this one morning the guy calls me, and he said, "April, do you have a butterfly this morning?" I told him to hold on and managed to get up and look and there on that ledge I saw this wet spot and a little speck of blood but no butterfly, and I thought "Oh dear God in heaven, the cat got it." I picked up the phone to tell this guy and just then suddenly I spotted it under the dressing table, it was moving one wing. The cat had got at it, but it was still alive. So I told the guy and he got so upset and he said "Oh no—oh, God, no—don't you see that's a life—a living thing?" Well, I got dressed and took it to the park and put it on a rose, it was summer then and it looked like it was going to be all right—I think, anyway. But that man—I really felt damaged by him—awful—that was just cruel. I got home and I called him back and said, "Listen, I'm a living thing too, you shithead!" *(Pause)* I never saw him again.

8
"THE ART OF DINING"

THE ART OF DINING

BY TINA HOWE

A nearsighted, terrifically shy writer in her early thirties, Elizabeth Barrow Colt is afraid of food. Now she's sitting in a magical, elegant little restaurant, across from a man she's just met, an editor who wants to publish her stories and with whom she's falling in love. The first monologue takes place over soup, the second over the entrées (striped bass with shrimp mousse). Elizabeth has already spilled one bowl of soup on her crotch and passed her replacement bowl to her companion. She watches him eat but doesn't touch a morsel of her own meal.

ELIZABETH BARROW COLT: When I was young I never even saw my mother in the kitchen. The food just appeared at mealtime as if by magic, all steaming and ready to eat. Lacey would carry it in on these big white serving platters that had a rim of raised china acorns. Our plates had the same rim. Twenty-two acorns per plate, each one about the size of a lump of chewed gum. When I was very young I used to try and pry them off with my knife. . . . We ate every night at eight o'clock sharp because my parents didn't start their cocktail hour until seven, but since dinnertime was meant for exchanging news of the day, the emphasis was always on talking . . . and not on eating. My father bolted his food, and mother played with hers: sculpting it up into hills and then mashing it back down through her fork. To make things worse, before we sat down at the table she'd always put on a fresh smear of lipstick. I still remember the shade. It was called "Fire and Ice" . . . a dark throbbing red that rubbed off on her fork in waxy clumps that stained her food pink, so that by the end of the first course she'd have rended everything into a kind of . . . rosy puree. As my father wolfed down his meat and vegetables, I'd watch my mother thread this puree through the raised acorns on her plate, fanning it out into long runny pink ribbons . . . I could never eat a thing . . . "WAKE UP, AMERICA!" she'd trumpet to me. "You're not being excused from this table until you clean up that plate!" So, I'd take several mouthfuls and then when no one was looking, would spit them out into my napkin. Each night I systematically transferred everything on my plate into that lifesaving napkin. □□□ It's amazing they never caught on.

THE ART OF DINING

BY TINA HOWE

ELIZABETH BARROW COLT: Mealtime was much the same as it had always been . . . Father still talked a blue streak, Mother still mashed her food into a pink soup . . . and I still spit everything out into my napkin. But they were paper napkins now, and since I cleared the table, there was no chance of discovery. I breathed easier. What changed then, was the violence that went into the cooking before-hand . . . I never saw such bloodletting over meals! If she didn't nick herself while cutting the tomatoes, she'd deliberately slice a finger while waiting for the rice to boil. "Why bother cooking?" she'd cry, holding her bleeding hands under the faucet. "We'll all be dead soon enough!" . . . It was around this time that Mother was starting to get . . . suicidal . . . *(She starts to laugh)* Oh dear, I shouldn't laugh . . . it was just so . . . comical! You see, Mother was very comical. She wore hats all the time, great turban-type creations piled high with arti-ficial flowers and papier-mâché fruits. She wore them outside and she wore them in the house. She wore them when she cooked and when she ate . . . great teetering crowns that bobbed and jingled with every move . . . poor Mother . . . I don't know what it was that made her so unhappy . . . her menopause, her cocktails before dinner, some private anguish . . . but during this period, she used to threaten to kill herself. After another bloodstained dinner, she'd throw herself face down on our driveway and beg my father to put the car in reverse and drive over her. "Don't be ridiculous, dear," he'd say. But she meant it and would lie there sobbing, "PLEASE . . . DO IT!" It was a ritual we went through every night . . .

ROOSTERS

BY MILCHA SANCHEZ-SCOTT

The time is the present, the place the Southwest. Chata, "a fleshy woman of forty," Sanchez-Scott writes, "gives new meaning to the word blowsy. She has the lumpy face of a hard boozer." On the day her brother Gallo, a rooster breeder and fighter, is returning home from prison, she sits making tortillas with Gallo's wife, Juana. Juana prays that Gallo will come back and worries that he won't; Chata, meanwhile, instructs her in the sensual art of the tortilla.

CHATA: Look at this. You call this a tortilla? Have some pride. Show him you're a woman. ☐☐☐ Ah, you people don't know what it is to eat fresh handmade tortillas. My grandmother Hortensia, the one they used to call "La India Condenada" . . . she would start making them at five o'clock in the morning. So the men would have something to eat when they went into the fields. Hijo! She was tough. . . . Use to break her own horses . . . and her own men. Every day at five o'clock she would wake me up. "Buenos pinchi días," she would say. I was twelve or thirteen years old, still in braids. . . . "Press your hands into the dough," "Con fuerza," "Put your stamp on it." One day I woke up, tú sabes, con la sangre. "Ah! So you're a woman now. Got your own cycle like the moon. Soon you'll want a man, well this is what you do. When you see the one you want, you roll the tortilla on the inside of your thigh and then you give it to him nice and warm. Be sure you give it to him and nobody else." Well, I been rolling tortillas on my thighs, on my nalgas, and God only knows where else, but I've been giving my tortillas to the wrong men . . . and that's been the problem with my life. First there was Emilio. I gave him my first tortilla. Ay Mamacita, he use to say, these are delicious. Aye, he was handsome, a real lady-killer! After he did me the favor he didn't even have the cojones to stick around . . . took my TV set too. They're all shit . . .

TEENYTOWN

BY LAURIE CARLOS, JESSICA HAGEDORN, ROBBIE MCCAULEY

"Pork" is a discrete section from a complex performance text that melds traditional minstrel-show format with music, dance and multi-media visuals to explore racism in popular culture. Written and originally performed by Robbie McCauley, this piece was performed as an a cappella torch song with backup singers. Out of context—in an audition or acting class, for instance—it might be done very differently.

"Pork"
I once lost a friend from eating pork.
Everybody was hungry, it was a late-nite munch,
it was a soul-food restaurant, real commercial,
but conscious enough back then to ask if you wanted
beef or pork ribs.

We'd shared stories of old aunts and
other roots down South. Neither of us
had ever been dirt poor, she was younger,
had gotten further away, I was uncomfortable
with something about her ease in America.
When I said "pork" to the waiter, her eyes
went up outta sight. With serious Black bourgeoisie
nationalists back then, you didn't eat pork. I
wanted to say "I'm sorry, it was a slip of the tongue,
a bad habit, I'll change my order." But I didn't.
I wasn't ready to tear down the walls that had grown
up mortared between us . . .

I remember I was opening doors inside myself.
I remember that the sauce on the ribs was awful,
mainly ketchup, and there was no more conversation.

It was years before I gave up red meat altogether
for health reasons and years later that I was able

to say, "I am a Black *revolutionary* nationalist/in-
ternationalist, that the struggle is a protracted one,
we are all in it, and that many of the contradictions
are resol—va—ble."

STILL LIFE

BY EMILY MANN

*Cheryl is married to Mark and is the mother of his children. The vio-
lence he experienced and committed in Vietnam—and that he still
carries—pervades their life together. Sometimes, he beats her; other
times, the brutality is subtler. She speaks directly to the audience, as
if to an interviewer, in this testimonial-style play.*

CHERYL:
Every day before Thanksgiving
Mark does a spaghetti dinner, and this
is a traditional thing.
This is the one traditional bone Mark has in his body,
and I'd like to break it.

He has twenty to forty-five people come to this thing.
He makes ravioli, lasagna, spaghetti, meatballs,
three different kinds of spaghetti sauce:
shrimp, plain, meat sauce.
Oh, he makes gnocchi! He makes his own noodles!
And it's good.
He's a damn good cook for Italian food.
But you can imagine what I go through
for three weeks for that party
to feed forty people.
Sit-down dinner.
He insists it's a sit-down dinner.
So here I am running around
with no time to cook with him.

I'm trying to get enough shit in my house
to feed forty people sit-down dinner.
We heated the porch last year
because we did not have enough room to seat forty people.
And I run around serving all these slobs,
and this is the first year he's really charged anyone.
And we lose on it every year.
I mean, we lose, first year we lost three hundred dollars.
This dinner is a five-hundred-dollar deal.
I'm having a baby this November,
and if he thinks he's having
any kind of spaghetti dinner,
he can get his butt out of here.
I can't take it.
Pizzas! He makes homemade pizzas.
You should see my oven.
Oh my God! There's pizza shit everywhere.
Baked on.
And when it's over with,
he just gets up and walks out.
He's just done.
The cleanup is no big deal to him.
He won't even help.
He rolls up the carpets for his dinner.
People get smashed!
He's got wine everywhere, red wine.
It has to be red so if it gets on my rugs,
my rugs are ruined and my couch is ruined.
I've just said it so many times I hate it.
He knows I hate it.

9

"ONE HOME TO THE NEXT"

AS THE CROW FLIES

BY DAVID HENRY HWANG

Mrs. Chan, a Chinese woman in her seventies, has just sent her befuddled husband off to a daily game of golf he never plays, since he can't drive to get to the course and sold his car long ago. Meanwhile, she sits alone, awaiting a ghost she's been warned will come for her. She's determined to fight and defeat it—to live.

CHAN: I arrive in America one day, June 16, 1976. Many times, I have come here before, to visit children, but on this day, I arrive to stay. All my friends, all the Chinese in the Philippine, they tell me, "We thought you are stupid when you send all your children to America. We even feel sorry for you, that you will grow old all alone—no family around you." This is what they tell me.

The day I arrive in America, I do not feel sorry. I do not miss the Philippine, I do not look forward live in America. Just like, I do not miss China, when I leave it many years ago—go live in Philippine. Just like, I do not miss Manila, when Japanese take our home during wartime, and we are all have to move to Baguio, and live in haunted house. It is all same to me. Go, one home to the next, one city to another, nation to nation, across ocean big and small.

We are born traveling. We travel—all our lives. I am not looking for a home. I know there is none. The day I was marry, my mother put many gold bracelets on my arm, and so many necklaces that the back of my head grows sore. "These," she tells me. "These are for the times when you will have to run."

AS THE CROW FLIES

BY DAVID HENRY HWANG

Hannah Carter is a sixty-year-old black woman who has been clean-ing house for the elderly Mrs. Chan for over ten years. Sandra Smith is Hannah's second self, in her forties; she likes a good, wild time and usually comes out (of Hannah) at night, ready to party. In truth, Sandra is a ghost who has come to take Mrs. Chan home—that is, out of this life. She speaks to Mrs. Chan.

SANDRA: You know, I've known Hannah—well, ever since she was a little girl. She wasn't very pretty. No one in Louisville paid much atten-tion to her. Yeah, she's had five husbands and all, okay, that's true, but my personal guess is that most of 'em married her because she was a hard-working woman who could bring home the bacon week after week. Certain men will hold their noses for a free lunch. Hannah thinks the same thing, though she hardly ever talks about it. How can she think anything else when all five of them left her as soon as they got a whiff of some girl with pipe cleaners for legs? Hard for her to think she's much more than some mule, placed on this earth to work her back. She spends most of her life wanderin' from one beautiful house to the next, knowing intimately every detail, but never layin' down her head in any of 'em. She's what they call a good woman. Men know it, rich folks know it. Everyplace is beautiful, 'cept the place where she lives. Home is a dark room, she knows it well, knows its limits. She knows she can't travel nowhere without returnin' to that room once the sun goes down. Home is fixed, it does not move, even as the rest of the world circles 'round and 'round, picking up speed.

TENNESSEE

BY ROMULUS LINNEY

Bent and ragged, with white hair unbound and wild, this old woman seems to live in the past and present at the same time: She's a girl of nineteen who left home with the first man who promised to take her across the mountains to Tennessee; and she's seventy years older, returning—for the first time—home.

OLD WOMAN: You hit it. Nineteen or ninety. That's me! Yes, sir. *(She steps off the porch. She stands in the yard, facing out, speaking to the family on the porch directly behind her)* When I was nineteen. I stood right here. Right where I'm standing now. And I wasn't no shriveled-up pea then. I was a choice item. The best-looking woman in these mountains. And the meanest. Mean and proud. Damn men. I didn't like 'em. Said so. Drove Momma crazy. You're wild, she said. Settle down. Like you? I said. Marry when you're a child. Work and slave for men who don't care one spit what you think or how you feel. Who never listen. Don't talk like that, Momma said, but I did. I give men hell. They'd come, and I'd spit, and they'd go. You didn't like it, either. You, you up there. You didn't. *(She is speaking to the family without looking at them, as if, now, they are her own)* Ab and Billy. Rachel and Poppa. Momma. You don't know what to do, do you? You just sit there, shake your heads. Watch me fight. Damn men. *(She stands straighter. She strokes her white hair)* Heavy-footed, tongue-tied, bug-eyed horsefaces, coming here looking for a slave. Wanting to lie on top of me one minute, and work me to death the next. And take me away from you. And you hoping one of them would. Clucking your tongues, saying, "Lands sakes, what will become of her, treating men like this." Wanting me to go. Well, I won't! I won't leave this house, and you, to be plowed under like dirt by some sweating, groaning, boneheaded man! Hell, no! *(She stares offstage. She sees someone coming)* And then, he came by. Griswold Plankman, the joke of the world. He came my way.

10

"I THOUGHT MY HEART WOULD BURST"

APPROACHING ZANZIBAR

BY TINA HOWE

An extraordinary and magical woman, the eighty-one-year-old Olivia is an eminent artist who creates massive, site-specific artworks in places of natural splendor. Now on her literal deathbed, she is visited by her nine-year-old grandniece, Pony. As the girl, haunted by dreams of death and dying, crawls in beside Olivia, the old lady reaches for a memory of intense life. When this speech concludes, she rises on the bed with Pony and, calling out the names of places around the world, begins to bounce high into the air.

OLIVIA *(Waking, groggy)*: I just had the most beautiful dream. □□□ I was on a train somewhere between Paris and Tangier . . . we'd stopped at some godforsaken town in the middle of nowhere, and standing on the platform was the most beautiful man I'd ever seen—tall, with olive skin and a thrilling mouth. He wore a white suit and was pacing up and down the platform carrying this enormous bouquet of poppies that stained his face crimson. I couldn't take my eyes off him. He was like something out of *The Arabian Nights*. I kept expecting to see peacocks and jeweled elephants stamping in the distance. Finally he caught my gaze . . . I pressed my face against the window and whispered, "My name is Callisto!" *(She laughs)* Do you believe it? I used to call myself Callisto in those days. . . . The train suddenly started up. We pulled out of the station. I watched him get smaller and smaller. Then I fell into a deep sleep. I began having nightmares . . . I was being chased down this long tunnel . . . I started to scream. Someone grabbed my hands. I opened my eyes. It was him! He'd jumped on the train at the last minute and was sitting across from me, eyes laughing, poppies blazing. . . . He didn't speak a word of any language I knew, but he held me spellbound. I never made it off the train. He wrapped me in his flying carpet and wouldn't let me go. You've never seen such feverish carryings-on. . . . He rocked me over mountains, sang me through rain forests and kissed me past ancient cities. Oh, what a ruckus we made! Well, you'll do it too, you'll do it all, wait and see. We ended up in Zanzibar, island of clovers. *(She removes her nasal cannula)* I was so full of him, I thought my heart would burst. Zanzibar!

ANNULLA

BY EMILY MANN

A young woman, fresh out of college and in search of oral histories from Eastern Europe, encounters Annulla Allen in her clean but chaotic home in England. Annulla is "seventy-four years old, Eastern European. Tiny. She never walks, she runs." She "prides herself on the fact that she has perfect English, which we know, of course, she doesn't." Annulla recounts her experiences of World War II when she escaped the Holocaust by posing as an Aryan; her husband, Gustav, was interned in Dachau and then, miraculously, released.

ANNULLA: During those thirteen months when I was alone, posing as an Aryan every day, I lost myself. I couldn't work. I got those crying fits. You know, they are called *schreikrampf,* screaming spasms. I suddenly screamed without any reason. I would be doing something normal, something ordinary, like ironing a shirt, and then suddenly I would get this screaming fit. That grief was so deep. Because I never believed that he would come back. *(Pause)* I met him on the stairs. I was in a coffeehouse in Vienna with some other women. They telephoned me to the coffeehouse and said, "Come quickly, there is news from Gustav." They did not want to shock me too much by telling me he had come back.

So I came up the stairs, and he came towards me down the stairs. You know, I was stunned! I was standing there, I couldn't move. I didn't believe my eyes. I thought I would never see him again. But my husband was such a good soul with such a mild nature that not even the Nazis could have harmed him. *(A laugh)* It is six years since he died and there are times I feel how long it has been since I saw him. ☐☐☐ You know, if his mother had not died from cancer, he would have never have got married. He had a slight Oedipus condition, my husband. When his mother died, she died a year before we got married, he felt suddenly completely lost. I married him, you know, only because I got so bedazzled by sex. And at this time, you couldn't sleep with a man like now. That was not done. Not in our circle. That is why I couldn't write my thesis. I was too absentminded, distracted by this sex. In Vienna, don't forget the men were all killed off in the First World War. There was one man to ten women in the 1920s. "So, all right," I said, "I'll marry him." He was very nice to me. As he always was. And he was very tender . . . And he wanted to get married by hook or crook. □□□ So, I got married.

SLEEP DEPRIVATION CHAMBER

BY ADAM P. KENNEDY AND ADRIENNE KENNEDY

"On Friday night, January 11," writes Suzanne Alexander, a prominent African-American playwright and author, "my son, a fine citizen who has never been in any trouble whatsoever, was knocked to the ground and beaten in the face, kicked repeatedly in the chest and stomach and dragged in the mud by an Arlington, Virginia, policeman whose name is Holzer. This occurred in his father's front yard on Riverdale Street in Arlington. My son was stopped because he had a taillight out on his car." The nightmarish aftermath of this beating and its subsequent trial propels Suzanne to write letter after letter in Teddy's defense and as a means of coping. These two appeals—to her daughter and to the governor of Virginia—appear below as they do in the play, one after the other.

SUZANNE:
Dear Patrice,

I can tell Edelstein thinks I may jeopardize Teddy's case by writing too many letters. He told me to write two: one to the governor and one to the county manager. I have written seventeen, but I haven't told him.

I begged him to tell me about the detective he said he uses. I asked him was it possible for me to talk to the detective. I wanted to find out where the policeman lives. I wanted to see the policeman who dragged my son in the mud.

I could tell Edelstein had begged Teddy not to tell me too many details.

"You're too emotional, Mrs. Alexander," he said, as we walked through his glass offices. He said he's afraid I may do something foolish. He judged me for being a mother. "I'm sorry I cried in your glass offices," I said.

Patrice, whatever happened about the detective who was supposed to investigate the policeman and his past? He must have found something. This policeman must have beat other people. There's no place I can go and get that information.

Dear Governor Wilder:

This is my final telegram to you. I'm still in Cleveland rehearsing my play about my years at Ohio State. Every day when I come to the Ohio Theatre I think of my father and brother. I pass their graves in Lakeview Cemetery.

I also think of my brother-in-law, March Alexander. I'm sure you've heard of him, Professor Emeritus at Stanford. He lives in a cottage by Lake Lagunita on the campus. He vanished again last week through the arch of eucalyptus trees, vanished. His depression about the conditions of African-Americans has worsened. Sometimes he sits in the sun near the Leland Stanford Chapel. (Stanford offers him economic security for life) yet the columns of the Quad, the golf course, the Palo Alto hills have become a source of melancholy to him. I know you must remember he was one of the first blacks to go to Africa to live. Now he has many illnesses.

I seek your help once more because my daughter Patrice (a lecturer at Stanford) called. She said Teddy told her not to tell me but the district attorney said Teddy may be denied the trial with judge. And we will have to wait several months for a trial by jury and Teddy said they know we fear a trial by jury. Juries tend to side with the police and the police would be sure to have secret witnesses. I have written to the county manager, the police chief, the NAACP. Can you help my son?

EARLY DARK

BY REYNOLDS PRICE

It's 1957. The twenty-year-old Rosacoke Mustian recalls the moment she met Wesley, the boy she's loved for seven years. In the three years he's been gone on a tour of duty in the navy, she has never stopped waiting for him with a conviction and single-mindedness her family and friends find strange and, potentially, self-destructive. Now he's due back any minute. "He's what I want," she tells her mother as this scene begins. "He's always been."

ROSACOKE: You had punished me for laughing that morning in church, and I wanted to die—which was nothing unusual—but guessed I could live if I breathed a little air, so I picked up a bucket and walked to the woods to hunt some nuts and win you back. It was getting on late. I was hoping you were worried. I was past Mr. Isaac's in the really deep woods. The leaves were all gone, but I hadn't found a nut. Still I knew of one tree Mildred Sutton had showed me—I was headed for that—and I found it finally. It was loaded—pecans the size of sparrows—and in the top fork a boy, a stranger to me. I was not even scared. He seemed to live there, twenty yards off the ground, staring out dead-level. I said "Are you strong enough to shake your tree?"—"If I wanted to," he said. I said "Well, want to please; I'm standing here hungry." He thought and then braced his long legs and arms and rocked four times—pecans nearly killed me. I rummaged round and filled my bucket, my pockets. He had still not faced me; so I said "Don't you want to share some of my pecans?" Then he looked down and smiled and said "I heard they were God's." I said "No, really they belong to Mr. Isaac Alston. He can't see this far."—"I can see him," he said. "You may can see Philadelphia," I said—he was looking back north—and he nodded to that but didn't look down. "How old are you?" I said. He said "Fifteen" and shut up again. "I'm thirteen," I said. He said "You'll live" and smiled once more toward Philadelphia and I came on home. I wanted him then and every day since.

ASSASSINS

BY STEPHEN SONDHEIM AND JOHN WEIDMAN

Lynette ("Squeaky") Fromme is one of fourteen Americans who have tried, successfully or un-, to assassinate a president. In Sondheim and Weidman's musical, Fromme aims to shoot President Gerald Ford as a way of proving herself worthy of the man she worships, Charles Manson.

FROMME: I was like you once. Lost. Confused. A piece of shit. □□□ Then I met Charlie. . . I was sitting on the beach in Venice. I'd just had a big fight with my daddy about, I don't know, my eye make-up or the bombing of Cambodia. He said I was a drug addict and a whore and I should get out of his house forever. □□□ I went down to the beach and sat down on the sand and cried. I felt like I was disappearing. Like the whole world was dividing into two parts. Me, and everybody else. And then this guy came down the beach, this dirty-looking little elf. He stopped in front of me and smiled this twinkly devil smile and said, "Your daddy kicked you out." He knew! "Your daddy kicked you out!" How could he know? My daddy didn't tell him, so who could've? *God.* God sent this dirty-looking little elf to save a little girl lost on a beach. He smiled again and touched my hair and off he went. And for a minute I just watched him go. Then I ran and caught his hand, and till they arrested him for stabbing Sharon Tate, I never let it go.

▌▌ "HE GOT SICK"

JACK

BY DAVID GREENSPAN

Three female speakers, illuminated to appear like "floating busts,"
recall the life of a man named Jack. They narrate in overlapping, par-
tial and mostly unpunctuated sentences. Here "1" speaks alone,
focusing on the facts of Jack's illness (AIDS is implied though not
named) and death.

1: And so Jack got ill he got sick and that that that's it plain and simple there's not much to say beyond that what can I what are you
what are you going to say listen it's not so much a question of why
he got sick or how he got sick I couldn't tell you what who's going
to who know how he got a million different opinions from this one
from that one too much drinking from that one too much smoking
from this one too much screwing around and around your head could
spin with all the what do these people no I don't know what can I
say for all I know they're all right for heaven's sake but who cares you
think I care you think well Jack doesn't care anymore he's dead for
heaven's sake he's buried or burned or I don't know I think he was
cremated either way he doesn't care unless there's what life after listen I'm not going to get into that kind of no I'm not going to get started
on that would be the end of who knows he got sick is what's important and the fact that now and this is important he didn't no he
didn't tell any no he didn't tell a soul he didn't breathe a word of it
to anyone but well there was one no one maybe two people he told
for spite he told them over and over and over again how unfair and
how goddamn unjust that he of all people should be struck down he
said it was shit that life was shit that life was fucked over and over
again he blamed it on this and that and this went on and on and on
and no one knew why he left town that summer he went to California
to a what some kind of natural healing with herbs and meditation he
hated it so he settled in Los Angeles of all places Los Angeles as if
there he would find health as if there he finally committed suicide

after a year or so I think maybe less than a maybe a whole year I
don't know.

Thank god by then he had seven tumors on the brain he had well
over a hundred lesions and he was driving everybody crazy. He was
driving everybody what do you think this experience made a better
person out of him he was horrible yelling and screaming and blaming and

AS IS

BY WILLIAM M. HOFFMAN

*Functioning as a kind of Greek chorus for this important early AIDS
play, the "dowdy, middle-aged" hospice worker introduces and, here,
concludes the action of the play. She works at Saint Vincent's
Hospital in New York City "to ease the way for those who are dying."
A former nun with a lively gallows humor and "a touch of the crank
about me," she has just closed a bed curtain around Rich, a writer
with AIDS, and his lover, Saul, enabling them to make love in Rich's
hospital room.*

HOSPICE WORKER: I have a new AIDS patient, Richard. He still has a
lot of denial about his condition. Which is normal. I think most of us
would go crazy if we had to face our own deaths squarely. He's a
wonderful man. He writes extraordinarily funny poems about the ward.
His lover's there all the time, and he's got a lot of friends visiting, and
both families. I only hope it keeps up. It's only his second time in the
hospital. They get a lot of support at first, but as the illness goes on,
the visitors stop coming—and they're left with only me.

But something tells me it's not going to happen in his case. You
should see how his lover takes care of him. God forbid they treat Rich
badly, Saul swoops down and lets them have it. He's making a real
pain in the ass of himself, which is sometimes how you have to be
in this situation.

Rich should be out of the hospital again in a week or so. For a while. He's a fighter. . . . The angry phase is just about over and the bargaining phase is beginning. If he behaves like a good little boy, God will do what Rich tells Him to do. . . . I certainly hope that God does.

I don't know anymore. Sometimes I think I'm an atheist. No. Not really. It's more that I'm angry at God: how can He do this? *(Pause)* *I* have a lot of denial, *I* am angry, and *I* bargain with God. I have a long way to go towards acceptance. Maybe it's time for me to resign. Maybe I'm suffering from burnout.

But what would I do if I didn't go to St. Vincent's? And it's a privilege to be with people when they are dying. Sometimes they tell you the most amazing things. The other night Jean-Jacques—he's this real queen, there's no other word for it—he told me what he misses most in the hospital is his corset and high heels. I mean he weighs all of ninety pounds and he's half dead. But I admire his spirit. The way they treat him. Sometimes they won't even bring the food to his bed. And I'm afraid to complain for fear they take it out on him! Damn them! . . . I've lost some of my idealism, as I said. Last night I painted his nails for him. *(She shows the audience her vividly painted fingernails)* Flaming red. He loved it.

THE FATHER

BY BEATRICE ROTH

Part poem and part prayer, this fragment comes from a continuous monologue, originally enacted by the author, spoken over objects on a table, arranged as if for a Jewish sabbath. During this passage, for instance, Roth poured sand from a peanut-butter jar into a crystal urn and, when the words were done, let the sand run out in silence. The man in the hospital bed is her father, a devout Jewish shopkeeper at the end of his sixty-year life.

In a strange bed in a hospital in a strange city
brought for one of medicine's more arrogant experiments
they vigil with him.
One August afternoon she and he alone receive a local rabbi

sent for to say Tilim with him. The rabbi stands beside the bed
small next to the outstretched fingers held rigid by a needle
   conducting
glucose through a transparent tube attached to a pouch above the
   bed.
The rabbi stands
a stranger here to perform an act of intimacy.
The father's smile quavers firmly
to put the stranger at his ease.
It goes unanswered.
The glucose persists shimmying downward pressing the reluctant
   vein.
The litany begins.
The rabbi's voice is thin.
The father's unwavering in its wavering.
The rabbi's words inaudible, eyes lidded by embarrassment.
The father bypasses this licensed emissary
his voice a feather each strand articulate faintness.
Suddenly the transparent tube shudders.
The glucose shimmies backward up the tube defying gravity.
That other tube leading from a fading intellect is lit by a beam begun
aeons earlier—a flash so dazzling, the vein spits the unnatural fluid
back into its desperate channel.
The father's eyes burn black.
Singed by a current
propelling his spirit.
Days later hurried break for sandwich luncheon
detained by table service busy harassed waitress
brother-in-law chiding sister for her sadness
rush back stand a moment in the doorway
he is asleep.
One step takes you to his side.
Kiss his forehead.
It is warm

                         remains warm for your kiss
                         though he is far beyond

Bent over
your brother stands sobbing in the bathroom.
Bent over
your brother is bleeding on a Korean field.

12
"DO BUSINESS WITH THE DEVIL"

A BRIGHT ROOM CALLED DAY

BY TONY KUSHNER

A featured actress in the German film industry during the years of Hitler's rise to power, Paulinka Erdnuss is on her way to becoming a minor star. Although she later makes an instinctive stab at resistance, she appears throughout the play as a compliant, almost indolent narcissist and opium user. She seems to see herself this way, too, believing that, in the face of real evil, she'd acquiesce without hesitation.

PAULINKA: I've seen Him. Well, not Him, exactly, or . . . When I had just started acting I did two seasons at the Municipal Theatre of Karlsruhe. Ever been to Karlsruhe? *(She smiles; it is a telling smile)* We were giving *Faust, Part One*, a play I've always detested, and I was playing Gretchen, a part I've always detested, and I was not happy, not happy at all. There were nights I thought I'd be stuck in the provinces forever, never see Berlin, never see the inside of a film studio, die, go to hell, and it'd be exactly like Karlsruhe. Black nights, you could imagine your whole life gone . . . You know the scene in the play where the black poodle turns into the Devil and offers Faust the world? All that demurring, endless, always seemed so coy to me. Just. . . . But so one night I was walking home after a performance and a very strange thing happened. I found myself going down a narrow street, an alley, really, one I'd never been down before, and suddenly. . . . There was this little black poodle, sitting on a doorstep. Waiting for me. Staring at me with those wet dark dog eyes. And I thought to myself: "It's Him! He's come to talk to me!" He's going to stand up on His little hind legs and say "Paulinka! Fame, films, and unsurpassable genius as an actor in exchange for your immortal soul!"
And that's when I knew it, and my dears I wish I didn't know: I'd never resist. I couldn't. I am constitutionally incapable of resisting anything. A good actress, a good liar, but not in truth a very good person. Just give me Berlin, sixty years of success, and then haul me off to the Lake of Fire! Do business with the Devil.

But the poodle had other things in mind. I guess I must have startled it when I asked it if it wanted to make me an offer. It *leapt* up at me, barking and snarling and obviously out for blood. Chased me for blocks. I escaped by ducking into a bar, where I drank and drank and drank . . .

Probably just somebody's nasty black poodle. But I've always wondered . . . what if it really was Him, and He decided I wasn't worth it?

FILM IS EVIL: RADIO IS GOOD

BY RICHARD FOREMAN

Kate—also the name of the actress who originated this role in Foreman's own production—appears on film, midway through a play set in a radio studio. As she speaks, the scenery changes abruptly, from a couch to a lunch table with two elderly ladies to in front of a striped wall that rocks dizzily from side to side. Likewise, the play mixes media and frequently shifts tone. Kate's speech engages the philosophical argument at its heart: Film captures and glamorizes surface realities and sends the subliminal message that only what's photographed is real; it can never, however, penetrate beyond appearances to the many hidden truths of our existence and consciousness. Remember: Kate is on film and is conscious of being caught there.

KATE: Reading the text of my heart, I say to myself: "Oh, dear. I am exiled from real consciousness of seeing the sandwich as the sandwich." □□□ I am excluded from real consciousness of what you're telling me. Maybe I had better get away from this motion picture camera that records my image, and that exiles me from my own consciousness. Did you know that film—to film somebody—steals the soul? □□□ It does. It steals the soul. It steals the soul. People in touch with their own inner life understand. They understand that. I am excluded from real consciousness of seeing myself, even when I think I'm looking at myself. □□□ I am excluded from real consciousness of getting my bearings when I do my imagination exercises, because that's just a ploy I use when I find myself in a place that's real, even if it doesn't seem real. □□□ Oh dear. I am excluded from real consciousness of seeing and experiencing the place I am entering. I am excluded from real consciousness of experiencing the other people here with me.

GREENSBORO

BY EMILY MANN

On November 3, 1979, five protesters involved in a "Death to the Klan" rally in Greensboro, N.C., were shot and killed by a group of Nazis and Ku Klux Klan members. Greensboro *explores the event and its repercussions through documentary testimony from both sides. Signe Waller's husband, Jim, a doctor who'd quit full-time practice to devote more time to political and civil-rights activism, was murdered that day, about eighteen months after they'd gotten married.*

SIGNE: They said we widows weren't human. We had no feelings of grief. The press said look at that woman. She can stand over her dead husband's body and scream about the party. What they didn't hear me scream was: "I can't go on living without Jim." I really felt like I couldn't go on living. For at least a year it was a matter of total indifference to me whether I lived or died. However people treat you, they give you an identity. I had to deal with this monster image.

I was the one left holding the red banner. I was the lightning rod. It's funny because when I was a teenager, my nickname in summer camp was Lightning Rod. So I was put out there. I did it voluntarily. I was happy doing it. I wanted to take most of the flak that way for being the up-front communist.

What I'm afraid of now is the same prejudices are operating, just attaching to different people. I live in Milwaukee now. This guy Dahmer—you know about him. He raped, mutilated, killed his young male victims. He lured people to his apartment, took photographs of them both before and after, put their hearts, their skulls in his refrigerator, put their heads in acid, ate their hearts, their body parts, it's unbelievable, unbelievable. Anyway, I heard that one of his victims, somehow managed to get away. He was naked. Dahmer ran out after him. The boy had found a police officer, and Dahmer said to the cop: "Oh he's just upset." So the police officer gave him *back to Dahmer!* He just gave him to his killer. The cop's attitude was: "Oh, he's just some faggot."

I mean, once there are categories of people who do not qualify as having full human stature—whether they are gays or communist or black people or whoever they are—I mean, once you can separate humanity that way, then you have already created an entire framework in which you can practice all kinds of oppression on people. And you can get away with it. As soon as you have that less than human thing operating, boy, you can do anything to people. And I can understand that, having been communist.

GETTING OUT

BY MARSHA NORMAN

Marsha Norman describes the following characters this way: Arlene is "a thin, drawn woman in her late twenties who has just served an eight-year prison term for murder." Arlie, played by a different actress, "is the violent kid Arlene was until her last stretch in prison . . . Arlene's memory of herself." In other words, these two speeches explore the before and the after—the young future convict and the older woman who must kill her own violent self to survive.

ARLIE: So, there was this little kid, see, this creepy little fucker next door. Had glasses an somethin' wrong with his foot. I don't know, seven, maybe. Anyhow, ever time his daddy went fishin', he'd bring this kid back some frogs. They built this little fence around 'em in the backyard like they was pets or somethin'. An we'd try to go over an see 'em but he'd start screamin' to his mother to come out an git rid of us. Real snotty like. So we got sick of him bein' such a goody-goody an one night me an June snuck over there an put all his dumb ol' frogs in this sack. You never heared such a fuss. *(Makes croaking sounds)* Slimy bastards, frogs. We was plannin' to let 'em go all over

the place, but when they started jumpin' an all, we just figur[ ]
was askin' for it. So, we taken 'em out front to the porch[ ]
throwed 'em, one at a time, into the street. *(Laughs)* Some[ ]
hit cars goin' by but most of 'em jus' got squashed, you know, runned
over? It was great, seein' how far we could throw 'em, over back of
our backs an under our legs an God, it was really fun watchin' 'em
fly through the air then *splat (Claps hands)* all over somebody's car
window or somethin'. Then the next day, we was waitin' and this little kid comes out in his backyard lookin' for his stupid frogs and he
don't see any an he gets so crazy, cryin' and everything. So me an
June goes over an tells him we seen this big mess out in the street,
an he goes out an sees all them frogs' legs and bodies an shit all
over the everwhere, an, man, it was so funny. We 'bout killed ourselves laughin'. Then his mother come out and she wouldn't let him
go out an pick up all the pieces, so he jus' had to stand there watchin'
all the cars go by smush his little babies right into the street. I's gonna
run out an git him a frog's head, but June yellin' at me "Arlie, git over
here fore some car slips on them frog guts an crashes into you."
(Pause) I never had so much fun in one day in my whole life.

GETTING OUT

BY MARSHA NORMAN

ARLENE: This chaplain said I had . . . said Arlie was my hateful self
and she was hurtin' me and God would find some way to take her
away . . . and it was God's will so I could be the meek . . . the meek,
them that's quiet and good an git whatever they want . . . I forgit that
word . . . they git the earth. □□□ And that's why I done it. □□□ They
tol' me . . . after I's out an it was all over . . . they said after the chaplain got transferred . . . I didn't know why he didn't come no more till
after . . . they said it was three whole nights at first, me screamin' to
God to come git Arlie an kill her. They give me this medicine an
thought I's better . . . then that night it happened, the officer was in
the dorm doin' count . . . an they didn't hear nuthin' but they come
back out where I was an I'm standin' there tellin' 'em to come see,

real quiet I'm tellin' 'em, but there's all this blood all over my shirt an I got this fork I'm holdin' real tight in my hand . . . *(Clenches one hand now, the other hand fumbling with the front of her dress as if she's going to show Ruby)* this fork, they said Doris stole it from the kitchen an give it to me so I'd kill myself and shut up botherin' her . . . an there's all these holes all over me where I been stabbin' myself an I'm sayin' Arlie is dead for what she done to me, Arlie is dead an it's God's will . . . I didn't scream it, I was jus' sayin' it over and over . . . Arlie is dead, Arlie is dead . . . they couldn't git that fork outta my hand till . . . I woke up in the infirmary an they said I almost died. They said they's glad I didn't. *(Smiling)* They said did I feel better now an they was real nice, bringing me chocolate puddin'. ☐☐☐ I'd be eatin' or jus' lookin' at the ceiling an git a tear in my eye, but it'd jus' dry up, you know, it didn't run out or nuthin'. An then pretty soon, I's well, an officers was sayin' they's seein' such a change in me an givin' me yarn to knit sweaters an how'd I like to have a new skirt to wear an sometimes lettin' me chew gum. They said things ain't never been as clean as when I's doin' the housekeepin' at the dorm. *(So proud)* An then I got in the honor cottage an nobody was foolin' with me no more or nuthin'. An I didn't git mad like before or nuthin'. I jus' done my work an knit . . . an I don't think about it, what happened, 'cept . . . *(Now losing control)* people here keep callin' me Arlie an . . . *(Has trouble saying "Arlie")* I didn't mean to do it, what I done . . .

HOW I LEARNED TO DRIVE

BY PAULA VOGEL

*"Sometimes to tell a secret, you first have to teach a lesson,"
explains Li'l Bit as she embarks on a story that spans thirty years of
her life. This story moves backward and forward in time, unfolding as
a series of lessons: the dos and don'ts of driving, for instance, and
the instructive "a mother's guide to social drinking" (second monologue below). The secret Li'l Bit reveals: her sexual relationship from
ages eleven to eighteen with her Uncle Peck, a man in his forties. In
the first monologue, she is twenty-five and hasn't seen her uncle since
her freshman year in college. "A mother's guide . . ." frames an earlier scene in which Peck celebrates Li'l Bit's success on her driving
test by plying her with cocktails. The Greek Chorus (Mother)—one
of several "Greek chorus" roles—as she lectures, grows increasingly sloshed.*

LI'L BIT: A long bus trip to upstate New York. I settled in to read, when
a young man sat beside me. "What are you reading?" he asked. His
voice broke into that miserable equivalent of vocal acne, not quite
falsetto and not tenor, either. I glanced a side view. He was appeal-
ing in an odd way, huge ears at a defiant angle springing forward at
90 degrees. He must have been shaving, because his face, with a
peach sheen, was speckled with nicks and styptic.

"I have a class tommorow." I told him.

"You're taking a class?"

"I'm teaching a class. I'm an instructor—actually, I'm still writing
my thesis."

He concentrated on lowering his voice. "I'm a senior." The light
was fading outside; so perhaps he was. With a very high voice.

I felt him thinking hard, what casual question to ask. "What do you teach?"

"Theatre," I replied.

Now, when one as an older woman answers such a query with "public policy," do you think young men on buses think: "Oh boy. Easy lay"?

I felt his "interest" quicken. Five steps ahead of the hopes in his head, I slowed down, waited, pretended surprise, acted at listening, all the while knowing we would get off the bus, he would just then seem to think to ask me to dinner, he would chivalrously insist on walking me home, he would continue to converse in the street until I would casually invite him up to my room—and—I was only into the second moment of conversation and I could see the whole evening before me.

And dramaturgically speaking, after the faltering and slightly comical "first act," there was the very briefest of intermissions, and an extremely capable and forceful and *sustained* second act. And after the second act climax and a gentle denouement—before the postplay discussion—I lay there as a passive spectator, and I thought about you, Uncle Peck. Oh: oh—this is the allure. Being older. Being the first. Being the translator, the teacher, the epicure, the already jaded. This is how the giver gets taken.

HOW I LEARNED TO DRIVE

BY PAULA VOGEL

FEMALE GREEK CHORUS (MOTHER):
A mother's guide to social drinking:

A lady never gets sloppy—she may, however, get tipsy and a little gay.

Never drink on an empty stomach. Avail yourself fo the bread basket and generous portions of butter. *Slather* the butter on your bread.

Sip your drink, slowly, let the beverage linger in your mouth—interspersed with interesting, fascinating conversation. Sip, never . . . slurp or gulp. Your glass should always be three-quarters full when his glass is empty.

Stay away from "ladies" drinks: drinks like Pink Ladies, Sloe Gin Fizzes, Daiquiris, Gold Cadillacs, Long Island Iced Teas, Margaritas, Pina Coladas, Mai Tais, Planters Punch, Brandy Alexanders, Fuzzy Navels, Grasshoppers, White Russians, Black Russians, Red Russians, Melon Balls, Blue Balls, Blue Hawaiians, Green Arkansans, Humming-

birds, Hemmorrhages and Hurricanes. In short, avoid an~~y~~
sugar, or anything with an umbrella. Get your vitamin C
Don't order anything with Voodoo or Vixen in the title or s~~
tions in the name like Dead Man Screw or the Missionary~~

(She sort of titters)

Believe me, they are lethal. . . . I think you were conceived after
one of those.

Drink, instead, like a man: straight up or on the rocks, with plenty of
water in between. You're less likely to feel hung over, no matter how
much you've consumed, and you can still get to work the next morning, even on little or no sleep.

Oh, yes. And never mix your drinks. Stay with one all night long,
like the man you came in with: bourbon, gin, or tequila 'til dawn,
damn the torpedoes, full speed ahead! □□□

Don't leave your drink unattended when you visit the ladies' room.
There is such a thing as white slavery; the modus operandi is to spike
an unsuspecting young girl's drink with a "mickey" when she's left
the room to powder her nose.

But if you feel you have had more than your sufficiency in liquor,
do go to the ladies room—often. Pop your head out of doors for a
refreshing breath of the night air. If you must, wet your face and head
with tap water. Don't be afraid to dunk your head if necessary. A wet
woman is still less conspicuous than a drunk woman. *(The Female
Greek Chorus stumbles a little; conspiratorially)*

When in the course of human events it becomes necessary, go to
a corner stall and insert the index and middle finger down the throat
almost to the epiglottis. Divulge your stomach contents by such per-
suasion, and then wait a few moments before rejoining your beau
waiting for you at your table. Let him *wait*. I always have mints in my
purse for such emergencies, although it is not advisable to use this
method as a habitual dietary aid.

Oh, no. Don't be shy or embarrassed. In the very best of estab-
lishments, there's always one or two debutantes crouched in the corner stalls, their beaded purses tossed willy-nilly, sounding like cats in
heat, heaving up the contents of their stomachs. □□□

I wonder what it is they do in the men's rooms. □□□

Thanks to judicious planning and several trips to the ladies' loo,
your mother once out-drank an entire regiment of visiting British officers on a good-will visit to Washington! Every last man of them!
Milque-toasts! How'd they ever kick Hitler's cahones, huh? No match

for an American lady—I could drink every man in here under the table— □□□

As a last resort, when going out for an evening on the town, be sure to wear a skin-tight girdle, so tight that only a surgical knife or acetylene torch can get it off you—so that if you do pass out in the arms of your escort, he'll end up with rubber burns on his fingers before he can steal your virtue—

THE FILM SOCIETY

BY JON ROBIN BAITZ

The Blenheim School for Boys in Durban, South Africa, 1970. Nan's husband has been fired from teaching for his self-destructive attempts to radicalize the old school ways of this bone-deep conservative academy. As a result, Nan's in danger of dismissal, too, which would ruin them. She struggles here, in front of a class of boys, to teach what she believes, to provide an antidote to the terrorist violence she sees in the South African ruling class (as embodied by the hard-liner Hamish Fox, for whom she's substituting). The conflict is to open the class's eyes, to humanize them, without going too far.

NAN *(Addressing her class)*: When I asked for essays on the Zulus, I wasn't looking for detailed accounts of native laziness in your father's factory, Cleasby. Nor am I interested in your examination of native killing techniques. It's tired and I'm tired of it. It's as if your Africa were some kind of Atlantis, with drums and spears. It's not the one we're in. *(Pause)* I thought we might then, try these essays again? Somehow demythologized, okay? I was thinking—as I was reading them—I was thinking back, remembering, because my family had a number of maids as I was growing up. And there was a blur, a period of faces, names—I can't connect, but there was Edna. And she had been with us for some years—this good-natured, virtually invisible friend. Whose life was actually far more complicted than ours. My father did nothing, really. There was a vastness of leisure time, a morass. *(Pause)* And Edna had this husband who worked in the mines whom she saw with less and less frequency over the years. My mother found his presence—his dusty, coarse skin—upsetting, even if he was only to spend the night in the little room in the back. He was never actually forbidden; it was a kind of subtle discouragement. And—it was the same with her children—who had been cast out to the grandmother's little squash patch and mud hut in Zululand . . . somewhere where everyone might be reunited at Christmas for a couple of days or so. Eventually, the circumstances of this thwarted, enslaved life, all the wretchedness, made functioning as a human being harder and harder. *(Pause)* And of course, as it becomes harder to function as a human being, it makes being a good servant pretty much an impossibility. *(Pause)* She became moody. Forgetting to bathe, becoming, finally, something of a darkness in our home. And as Edna's personality became that of a toast-burning hag, I started to develop an intense dislike for her. There was a point where my family's main source of bored, wintry amusement—the height of morbidity, finally, was to, over dinner, discuss the decline of Edna, discuss it, in fact, as she served. *(Pause)* And, of course, she began to sour. Her humanness became overwhelming, like meat left out far too long. And when the dimension of her life overtook our own, she was finally, simply sent away. *(Pause)* And the next week, it began again with a new servant. So really, I mean, this kind of Atlantis you describe, it hardly does credit to the real one which has its own violence, its own terrors, quite independent of Fox's Africa of guns and war. That Africa—denies what we are. Our own brand of callousness. Surely there have been lives that have meant something to you? And I would very much like to know about that. Do you understand this?

THE CONDUCT OF LIFE

BY MARIA IRENE FORNES

Leticia's husband, a Latin American army lieutenant ten years younger than she is, has just informed her that she isn't in his will. He knows she'd give his money to the poor, a move he views as fool-

ish. She sees his action as proof that he doesn't love her, that she's no more to him than a "person who runs the house." She addresses him and, when he walks out, her best friend, another army man named Alejo.

LETICIA: If I had money I would give it to those who need it. I know what money is, what money can do. It can feed people, it can put a roof over their heads. Money can do that. It can clothe them. What do you know about money? What does it mean to you? What do you do with money? Buy rifles? To shoot deer? □□□ He has no respect for me. He is insensitive. He doesn't listen. You cannot reach him. He is deaf. He is an animal. Nothing touches him except sensuality. He responds to food, to the flesh. To music sometimes, if it is romantic. To the moon. He is romantic but he is not aware of what you are feeling. I can't change him.—I'll tell you why I asked you to come. Because I want something from you.—I want you to educate me. I want to study. I want to study so I am not an ignorant person. I want to go to the university. I want to be knowledgeable. I'm tired of being ignored. I want to study political science. Is political science what diplomats study? Is that what it is? You have to teach me elemental things because I never finished grammar school. I would have to study a great deal. A great deal so I could enter the university. I would have to go through all the subjects. I would like to be a woman who speaks in a group and have others listen.

14

"BRING BACK MEMORIES!"

PAINTING CHURCHES

BY TINA HOWE

While packing up her Beacon Hill home of many decades, Fanny Sedgwick Church, a woman from fine Boston stock, comes across her husband Gardner's old galoshes. Memories rush in. She's talking to her daughter, an artist who has returned to help with the move, and she's yelling for Gardner. He's out of the room, but Fanny always yells to him, wherever he is. She's convinced that he's "deaf as an adder."

FANNY: God, these bring back memories! There were real snow-storms in the old days. Not these pathetic little two-inch droppings we have now. After a particularly heavy one, Daddy and I used to go sledding on the Common. This was way before you were born. . . . God, it was a hundred years ago! . . . Daddy would stop writing early, put on these galoshes and come looking for me, jingling the fasten-ers like castanets. It was a kind of mating call, almost . . . *(She jingles them)* The Common was always deserted after a storm; we had the whole place to ourselves. It was so romantic. . . . We'd haul the sled up Beacon Street, stop under the State House, and aim it straight down to the Park Street Church, which was much further away in those days. . . . Then Daddy would lie down on the sled, I'd lower myself on top of him, we'd rock back and forth a few times to gain momentum and then . . . WHOOOOOOOOSSSSSSSSHHHHH . . . down we'd plunge like a pair of eagles locked in a spasm of love-making. God, it was wonderful! . . . The city whizzing past us at ninety miles an hour . . . the cold . . . the darkness . . . Daddy's hair in my mouth . . . GAR . . . REMEMBER HOW WE USED TO GO SLEDDING IN THE OLD DAYS? . . . Sometimes he'd lie on top of me. That was fun. I liked that even more. *(In her foghorn voice)* GARRRRRRRRRD-NERRRRR?

THE OLDEST PROFESSION

BY PAULA VOGEL

Five aged prostitutes sit on a park bench in New York City, shortly after the election of Ronald Reagan in 1980. Mae, the oldest at eighty-three, has enjoyed a long tenure as madam. She is "a leader who finds the management of men ridiculously easy, and has mastered the management of women as well." Never failing to protect her stable of ladies, she has just chased a young punk prostitute off their corner, shouting, "This has been our beat for over forty-five years, and listen, baby, we still tick!"

MAE: When a woman can't defend her territory or her girls, it's time to get out of the Life. I tell you, it makes me sad. When I see the new generation of prostitutes working right on the street—gypsies, all of them—on their own with no group, no house to call their own, no amenities for customers, no tradition or . . . or finesse . . . where's the pride in the name of prostitute? It's all gone downhill since the government poked their nose in our business and booted decent self-respecting businesswomen out of Storeyville. Remember the House where we all first met? A spick-and-span establishment. The music from Professor Joe in the parlor; the men folk bathed, their hair combed back and dressed in their Sunday best, waiting downstairs happy and shy. We knew them all; knew their wives and kids, too. It was always Mr. Buddy or Mr. Luigi; never this anonymous "John" for any stranger with a Jackson in his billfold. □□□ There was honor in the trade . . . My father went to Storeyville often when I was a girl. Mother used to nod to Miss Sophie right in the street before Mass in the Quarter. Miss Sophie saved our lives, she did. The depression of '97—Papa lost work and there were seven of us to feed. So every morning before folks were up and about, Miss Sophie came and put groceries on the back step—Papa was regular customer, she couldn't let us starve. And none of the neighbors knew a thing. Finally Papa got work again; the money came in for food on the table and Saturday nights at Miss Sophie's. And then my mother got pregnant again—I guess there was plenty of my father to go around. Mother had a boy. So Miss Sophie said she'd be real pleased if they named that boy after her gentleman protector.

THE OLDEST PROFESSION

BY PAULA VOGEL

Like Mae (above), Edna loves her work. She's a "good-time girl" and, at a mere seventy-four years old, one of the youngest prostitutes working for Mae when the play begins. Now that Mae and two senior hookers have died, she suddenly finds herself a madam or, as she says, "management," a position that doesn't feel right to her. She's got some doubts and regrets; she's thinking about things.

EDNA: Sometime Mr. Benjamin acts just like a child when it's time to leave. He holds me around the waist and says he's not going to let me out of his sight. Then I have to slap his face, and say, "Mr. Benjamin, let go this instant. What makes you think any woman would have you?" And I rub the bristle on his face and say, "Shave this mug!" And then he rubs his beard on my face and I scream. And sometimes he says, "Edna, you've got to marry me! I can't afford to keep this up . . ." He doesn't really mean it, though. It's just one of our games . . . he's my good-time papa, that's what I call him. I like to sit on his knee and put my hands under his shirt; I like his smell—I know it after all these years. There was a time when he was still working on Wall Street that Mae would schedule me in regular for him at lunch time; I had the key to his apartment. He'd come through the door, three-piece suit and briefcase, and say "What's for lunch?" And I'd jump on him and wrap my legs around him . . . He's got a picture of himself in uniform on the night table, twenty-five years old and smiling. Gives me the willies to look at it. I don't like to think of Mr. Benjamin as a young man. It makes me sad. Don't you think young men are awfully sad?

15

"YOU WAIT ALL YOUR LIFE FOR SOMETHING GOOD TO HAPPEN AND THEN IT DOES!"

ANTEROOM

BY HARRY KONDOLEON

The play is nearly over when Barbara enters for the first time, in search of her son, Wilson (Will). A rough woman of at least forty with "dyed hair and coarse, contemporary casual clothing," she's thoroughly out of sync with the Southampton, Long Island, mansion in which Wilson has been working as a butler and in whose anteroom she now stands. Barbara's just gotten married and wants her son to come home. She's talking to the first person she finds.

BARBARA: Holy Moly. Look at all this silver! You're not Maya, are you? □□□ She told me I should come for my son Will which is what I wanted to do anyway but you know kids when you get remarried, what are you wearing? Anyway, so I drove with my boyfriend—actually my husband! As of recently. I mean, you know, you wait all your life for something good to happen and then it *does!* What a kick! I am crazy for this guy—he's younger than I am—I know that doesn't matter at all nowadays and I look much younger than I am but I thought let them see you have a child half grown and they'll think you've got to be a Methuselah or something I'm telling you so who could blame me keeping Will a secret but when I told Tom he was flabbergasted I had a son—thrilled—go figure it, you can't predict things.
(A car horn honks.)
He's going to be a good disciplinarian too, Tom. □□□
(The car horn again.)
That's Tom, not too patient! I should get your numbers, Labor Day we're going to have a big barbecue. What is this room anyway? I thought I passed through the kitchen on the way in. Doesn't matter. Just between us I'll tell you something. It wasn't easy for me. Okay? I had a young son to raise and a husband who liked the booze and did a disappearing act—no one wanted to know me from *Adam*. Why am I saying this? Because I have been down *twice* in my life and no one came to help me. Not family, not friends, certainly not family! I

have a word to the wise—it's not too good to be too good in this world because they *fuck* you, excuse my French but they *fuck* you and then they *fuck* you again! I used to be a chain smoker. I gave it up for two years then I thought *what the fuck for? (She lights a cigarette quickly and takes a long drag on it)* Roll with the punches they say. You know what I say? Fuck 'em. Why should I have them over for dinner? Now if I have them over at all I have them for drinks. No more lamb chops and no more candy! You're nice ladies so take my advice, it doesn't pay to be nice. *Take my advice:* THINK ABOUT YOU. Let me shake your hands.

THE LOMAN FAMILY PICNIC

BY DONALD MARGULIES

In a high-rise apartment in Coney Island, Brooklyn, circa 1965, with a picture window looking out on an identical high-rise, the thirty-eight-year-old Doris sits, wearing a housecoat over her pajamas. She's making her Halloween costume—the Bride of Frankenstein—by shredding her wedding dress with a pair of scissors.

DORIS: On the day I was married the world showed every sign of coming to an end. It rained—no, poured. Thunder. Cracks of lightning. Big Pearl S. Buck tidal waves. You get the picture. Did I turn back? Did I cancel? Did I say never mind, no thank you? A good omen, my mother told me. There had never been such a terrifying convergence of weather post-Noah; a good omen. Hail, did I mention hail? Like my mother's matzo balls falling from the sky shouting *Don't! Don't!* each time a *knaidel* smacked the roof of the rented limo. A better omen still, my mother said, hail. What about sunshine?, Momma?, I asked, what about a sunny wedding day? Also a good omen, my mother said. *(A beat)* I began to distrust her. *(A beat)* Two seconds in my wedding dress: splattered with mud. I should've known. Look at this: ruined. From day one. *(Points to various stains)* Mud, rain, hail, locusts, boredom, moraine . . . *(Looking directly at us)* I love the way my life has turned out. I have two wonderful boys. Mitchell is my baby. He's eleven. And Stewie is gonna be bar mitzvahed next Saturday at ten in the morning, to be followed by a gala affair starring me. What boys I have! I'm very lucky, knock on Formica. Smart?! Mitchell has a reading level, goes off the charts. So smart are my boys. Their father is not at all threatened by how smart they are. They aren't showoffs. I don't like showoffs. I raised my boys to stand out but not too much, you know?, otherwise people won't like you anymore. Look what happened to the Jews in Europe. Better you should have friends and be popular, than be showy and alone. My Aunt Marsha may she rest in peace taught me that. She was very popular. *(A beat. Refers to the wedding dress)* Last night was my wedding anniversary. Eighteen years. Herbie had to work, what else is new. I love the way my life has turned out. Did I say that already? On the day I was married the world showed every sign of coming to an end. . . .

AND BABY MAKES SEVEN

BY PAULA VOGEL

"The end of a very long day": Ruth has just returned from the ordeal of watching her lover, Anna, give birth. They plan to raise the child together, with the help of their roommate, Peter, the baby's biological father. After a moment of listening to the empty apartment, Ruth speaks to Peter.

RUTH *(Quietly)*: He looks just like you.
  (Beat.)
  I guess Anna and I really started talking about having a child after our first year together. You know how it is, that first year . . . you spend every moment in side glances at your lover, learning this new alphabet—her face, her walk, her gestures . . . the way she holds a pen, the way she chews the inside of her cheek in concentration; how her left nostril flares ever so slightly when she's amused—and you feel so ardent, you're in first grade all over again, in love with your teacher—so much in love that you wake early to study this alphabet while she's still asleep, memorizing her face on the pillow . . .

And I used to imagine that somewhere in the United States, there must be a pioneer geneticist, a woman in a lab coat we could go to, who would take some DNA from Anna and some DNA from me—and she'd combine us in a petri dish in a little honeymoon culture at just the right temperature—and then this growing synthesis would be transplanted in one of us, and when he or she would emerge, nine months later—the baby would have Anna's eyes winking beneath my eyebrows.

But finally I thought—well, I can always see my own face anytime I want to in the mirror. But I could see Anna's face at birth, Anna in diapers, a little Anna coming home from school. Or if the baby was born a boy—even better—I'd see his Adam's apple grow beneath her chin, or I'd experience that awkward moment right before puberty, before his voice changes, when I mistake his hello on the phone for hers—

Well. I guess I didn't think this all the way through.

16

"DREAMING AHEAD"

ANGELS IN AMERICA: PERESTROIKA

BY TONY KUSHNER

This scene comes near the end of the second half of Angels in America. *Harper, an agoraphobic and valium-popping "Jack (flawed) Mormon," has just left her husband. Her earlier escapes, by means of pills and episodic fantasies, have spirited her from Antarctica to the principalities of heaven. Her final flight, though, is real. She has said good-bye to Joe, a ruined marriage and presumably fear and barbituates as well. Armed with a single credit card and a kind of rock-bottom truth that comes with loss, she now heads west.*

HARPER: Night flight to San Francisco. Chase the moon across America.

God! It's been years since I was on a plane!

When we hit thirty-five thousand feet, we'll have reached the tropopause. The great belt of calm air. As close as I'll ever get to the ozone.

I dreamed we were there. The plane leapt the tropopause, the safe air, and attained the outer rim, the ozone, which was ragged and torn, patches of it threadbare as old cheesecloth, and that was frightening . . .

But I saw something only I could see, because of my astonishing ability to see such things:

Souls were rising, from the earth far below, souls of the dead, of people who had perished, from famine, from war, from the plague, and they floated up, like skydivers in reverse, limbs all akimbo, wheeling and spinning. And the souls of these departed joined hands, clasped ankles, and formed a web, a great net of souls, and the souls were three-atom oxygen molecules, of the stuff of ozone, and the outer rim absorbed them, and was repaired.

Nothing's lost forever. In this world, there is a kind of painful progress. Longing for what we've left behind, and dreaming ahead.

At least I think that's so.

NO MERCY

BY CONSTANCE CONGDON

Jackie is a thirty-five-year-old televangelist with "the sophistication in manner and dress of a female executive." Her preaching has been criticized as cold, but she has a firm, sincere belief that "a church should be built on the word" and not on Holy Roller theatrics. She eschews emotional outbursts, and so the one that lifts her to her feet at the end of this sermon disorients, confuses her.

JACKIE: Today we're looking at the Rapture, that moment when "we shall be changed, in the twinkling of an eye." Now the word *rapture* means—this is from Webster's Dictionary: □□□ "the state of being transported by lofty emotion; ecstasy or the transporting of a person from one place to another, especially to heaven." So plane, bus, train, or Rapture—all forms of transportation. □□□ What it is is the coming of Christ for the Church in which He instantly catches up all living believers to meet Him in the air and translates them into perfect and immortal bodies without them experiencing physical death. □□□ So you could be Raptured, like that, and someone is standing there looking at a pair of your empty shoes. □□□ There are signs leading up to the Rapture, of course. And these I was describing earlier this morning. But they are all part of the Tribulation—Armageddon being the climax of many years of suffering, war, natural disasters, droughts, world famines. And can any of us deny that these signs are present and increasing? All we need to do is watch the news, read the paper. And any of us then might pray that we might be Raptured before we have to witness any more suffering.

I, myself, many times think it should happen now because the world has had enough. When I see the faces of children who are starving because a drought has ravaged their country, or a war has ravaged their country, or I see bodies being removed from the site of an earthquake and people wandering, looking for a lost father or a daughter, I—planes with bombs over our heads right now! The leaders of the world . . . no one is doing anything, no one is listening. IT'S COMING. WHO'S READY? DEAR GOD.

THE CONDUCT OF LIFE

BY MARIA IRENE FORNES

The destitute, twelve-year-old Nena is kept in a basement and regularly raped by an army lieutenant commander in an unnamed Latin American country. It's not clear how long she's been locked up in his house. She appears onstage for the first time here. As she talks to the household servant, she sits at the kitchen table, separating stones from beans.

NENA: I used to clean beans when I was in the home. And also string beans. I also pressed clothes. The days were long. Some girls did hand sewing. They spent the day doing that. I didn't like it. When I did that, the day was even longer and there were times when I couldn't move even if I tried. And they said I couldn't go there anymore, that I had to stay in the yard. I didn't mind sitting in the yard looking at the birds. I went to the laundry room and watched the women work. They let me go in and sit there. And they showed me how to press. I like to press because my mind wanders and I find satisfaction. I can iron all day. I like the way the wrinkles come out and things look nice. It's a miracle isn't it? I could earn a living pressing clothes. And I could find my grandpa and take care of him. □□□ He sleeps in the streets. Because he's too old to remember where he lives. He needs a person to take care of him. And I can take care of him. But I don't know where he is.—He doesn't know where I am.—He doesn't know who he is. He's too old. He doesn't know anything about himself. He only knows how to beg. And he knows that only because he's hungry. He walks around and begs for food. He forgets to go home. He lives in the camp for the homeless and he has his own box. It's not an ugly box like the others. It is a real box. I used to live there with him. He took me with him when my mother died till they took me to the home. It is a big box. It's big enough for two. I could sleep in the front where it's cold. And he could sleep in the back where it's warmer. And he could lean on me. The floor is hard for him because he's skinny and it's hard on his poor bones. He could sleep on top of me if that would make him feel comfortable. I wouldn't mind. Except that he may pee on me because he pees in his pants. He doesn't know not to. He is incontinent. He can't hold it. His box was a little smelly. But that doesn't matter because I could clean it. All I would need is some soap. I could get plenty of water from the public faucet. And I could borrow a brush. You know how clean I could get it? As clean as new. You know what I would do? □□□ I would make holes in the floor so the pee would go down to the ground. And you know what else I would do? I would get straw and put it on the floor for him and for me and it would make it comfortable and clean and warm. How do you like that? Just as I did for my goat.

CLOUD TECTONICS

BY JOSÉ RIVERA

Celestina del Sol is a unearthly, beautiful woman in her twenties who, over the forty-year action of the play, doesn't age. She lives, it seems, outside of time. When Celestina first appears, waiting for a bus in the pouring rain, she has been pregnant for two years. She's picked up by a man named Aníbal, who shelters her from the Los Angeles floods in his modest house. There, she begins to talk about sex and the lover she's searching for, Rodrigo Cruz.

CELESTINA: I think about sex all the time, though I've only had one lover in my life, only one time. Rodrigo Cruz. And I almost had two! That despicable trucker who kept touching my knees. But I ran away from him. I took my chances in the rain. But even he couldn't stop my endless daydreaming and nightdreaming about sex: about Rodrigo's wrinkled back, my legs wrapped around his face . . . this obsession of mine . . . this tidal wave that started sometime when I was younger, when I lived in that one room. When Papi bought me a bicycle to give me something else to think about besides my body, and one glorious day I was allowed to ride around and around the house, because my Papi wanted me to count numbers, count numbers, over and over; he said it would teach me about the nature of "time," and I tried and tried. I really did, but I didn't learn anything, I was just so grateful to be outside my little room for once! *(Beat)*
Then Papi hired Rodrigo to work on his boat "The Celestina." And

I would stare at him from my window as he worked. He was beautiful. I wondered if I was in love. And he would look back at me and stare and his hair was so long and black. And I wondered is that what love looks like? And I don't know how many years passed . . . (I didn't know the word "years" then. I learned it on the road when the trucker taught me all kinds of words like "years" and "now" and "yesterday" and "minute" and "century") . . . and it must have been years . . . because years are longer than days (I learned this!) . . . and Rodrigo's hair was long and gray and he snuck into my room and did his dirty thing and left me . . . and my parents died in the other room and I went out to see because the house had grown so quiet and there they were in their little bed, holding hands, the green bedspread half covering their wrinkled bodies, they were naked and pale and covered in long gray hairs and very, very dead. That's the one time I stopped dreaming of sex when I called the police and told them Mami and Papi were dead, then I got dressed, and I lost all track of "time" and I got scared, and I ran out in the rain because I was sure they'd blame me and in my endless stay in my room I didn't learn much, but I learned by reading detective novels that when somebody dies the police always come to take you away and kill you with a lightning chair. That's when I hit the road, pregnant, looking for Rodrigo Cruz, angry and excited because he was the only man I ever had sex with and I keep thinking about sex with Rodrigo and I love the word "sex" and if I could fuck fuck fuck all day I would!

17

"WORLD WITHOUT END"

WORLD WITHOUT END

BY HOLLY HUGHES

The speaker—the author originally—is alone onstage, sometimes lounging in an overstuffed wing-backed chair. She's decked out in a "red silk off-the-shoulder number, possibly her mother's, and gold high heels." She speaks, for most of the extended monologue from which the piece below is excerpted, to the audience.

After my mother died, seven blue herons flew right over the top of the Holiday Inn and landed smack-dab in the middle of our front lawn. Meaning . . . you tell me. And after my mother died I was having this dream about my mother and she was drowning so I went in the water after her. And she just kept swimming farther and farther out, saying it was really silly for me to try to save her because I was the one who was drowning. After my mother died, I probably don't have to tell you this, but all of my sentences started with: "After my mother died . . . " And then, a little while after my mother died, the only thing I really wanted to do was fuck.

So there's this guy at work, right. Jeez! Always hovering over my PC asking me if I want to go to a Blarney Stone, right? So finally I said to him: "Look, I hate you. You're an idiot. I'm a lesbian. You touch me, you're a dead man, okay?"

And he's just laughing and laughing. I've never been so funny in all my life.

After my mother died, I told him that she had died. And he started to cry, I mean, he started to cry! I couldn't believe it. This idiot this dumbo I had yelled at fifty times a day to get out of my face was crying all over the copier about my mother.

And I thought: "Okay, sucker, maybe you're going to get lucky after all."

All of a sudden I knew what I wanted. I wanted to be nasty. I wanted to be nasty in Spanish, because if you're going to do it you might as well do it in Spanish, it sounds better: "*Sin vergüenza.*" I wanted to be desnuda in my terrarium with this junior account executive from

Middle Village Queens, I wanted to be outside of history, I wanted to rewrite the Bible, so I said, "Let's go to the Blarney Stone." We went there and we knocked back a few pink squirrels.

Then I took him . . . downtown.

On the Lexington Avenue local he detailed the various disgusting acts he was going to commit to my defenseless body and then he asked what I had in store for him.

I said: "Okay, cowboy. Here's the program. You're on the menu. We're going to go for broke, we're going to take the plunge. I have plans to rewrite the Bible and when I get through with you tonight, this is the way it's going to read from now on."

(She leans back in the chair. She slips into another world like she is slipping into a silk robe.)

Oh! They were naked at last.

Cara a cara entre azul y buenas noches.

Face to face between blue and holy nights.

Two ficus trees, two alley cats, two ancient jade plants growing out of the same straw hat. You could call this a walk-up Garden of Eden. And the first word spoken is: *"Ooh-la-la."*

THE MODEL APARTMENT

BY DONALD MARGULIES

Deborah visits her father from another world. Part dream, part wishful memory, she is his beautiful angel, haunting him. She died in a concentration camp, but her father has never left her behind. The play ends with this: Max, the father, asleep in a chaise lounge on a sundeck in Florida, Wall Street Journal *at his side, Deborah speaking to him.*

DEBORAH: I miss you at *Pesach, Tateh.* Everyone is there but you. We always talk about you. We do. We haven't forgotten. We wonder how you survived. Everyone is very old now, but healthy. Smashed bones are mended, muscles are restored. Hair has grown in nicely. Thick, shiny hair. And we've all put back the weight we lost, some of us *too* much. Everyone is dressed in their best, their fanciest clothes reserved for holy days. You should see. We look like ourselves again. A very handsome family. I'm still the youngest, so I get to ask the *feir kashas*. I let the boy cousins compete for the *afikoman*. I won't play with them. They're wild. They tease me and run around the living room. They're restless, I know. I am, too. But I like to stay with the men. Zaydie Duvid and Zaydie Schmuel conduct the seder together and argue about everything. The seder goes on into the night. I'm hungry, so hungry, but I can hardly keep my eyes open. The boys shriek and tug on my hair. Mameh and Bubbie Sura and Bubbie Bessie and Aunt Chaya and Aunt Rifke and Aunt Freyda—all the women—they all worry about the food, keeping the food fresh and warm. There is so much food! The kitchen is noisy with women. The dining room is cloudy with smoke and opinions. It's like it used to be when we were all together. No, it's noisier, there are more of us together now than there were before, so many of us. □□□ It's *Pesach* all the time, *Tateh*. I can't remember when it wasn't *Pesach*. I miss you all the time. The men are always arguing. And a feast is always awaiting us in the kitchen. And I'm always hungry, always hungry. And the boys are always running wild. And the arguing in the dining room goes on and on, into the night. And I can't keep my eyes open, I've sipped too much wine, and I don't want to go to sleep hungry, but my eyes are closing, they're closing, and I don't want to fall asleep and miss the feast, I don't want to miss the feast . . .

THE MOJO AND THE SAYSO

BY AISHAH RAHMAN

Three years ago today, Awilda Benjamin's ten-year-old son, Linus, was shot in the back by police while out walking with his father. The father—Awilda's husband—spends his time working on junkyard cars and avoiding the subject of the murder. Meanwhile, Awilda's alienation from him intensifies. Here, as she speaks to him, she handles the check they received yesterday—payment for the wrongful death of their child.

AWILDA *(Gingerly taking up check and looking at it)*: UGH. I hate to touch it. It feels . . . funny. It's got an awful smell too. It must be the paper they use nowadays to print these things. "Payment for Wrongful Death." Big digits. Now we got lots of money. Lots of money for the life of our boy. How do they figger? How do they know? How do they add up what a ten-year-old boy's life is worth to his parents? Maybe they have a chart or something. Probably feed it into a computer. Bzzzz. "One scrawny brown working-class boy. Enter. No wealthy relatives. Size 4 shoe. A chance of becoming rich in his lifetime if he plays Lotto regularly." How many dollars? How many cents? Do they know about the time I found out I was pregnant with him? My absolute joy that God has sent me this child. True, I already had Walter but that was before you. But you loved us anyhow and soon Linus was growing inside of me because we were in love. Yes, there was never enough money and we were always struggling but that's just the way life is. We knew we were supposed to have this baby. You took me to your mother and father and sisters and all your sisters, brothers, aunts and uncles. Your whole tribe. You told them, "This is my woman and she's going to have our child." They all hugged and kissed me. Do they know about the way you would put your head on my stomach and listen? Did they figger in the way you held my hand with tears in your eyes when I was in labor? When he was born the grandparents, aunts, uncles, neighbors and friends brought presents, ate and drank and danced and sang. Do they know about those moments? Did they add them in here? And what about Linus himself? He would make me throw out all my mean, petty, selfish parts and give him the best person I could be. Remember when he was good? Remember when he was bad? The times he was like us yet someone brand-new? And . . . what . . . about . . . what . . . he . . . might . . . have . . . been? How do they figger? How do they know?

THE MODEL APARTMENT

BY DONALD MARGULIES

"Neil will get a kick out of this," Lola says, before brightly launching into a story she's told so many times that her husband and daughter know it word for word. The storyteller and her audience make an unlikely pair: Lola, an Eastern European concentration-camp survivor now in her sixties, and Neil, fifteen, the mildly retarded, homeless black boyfriend of Lola's "obese, unkempt, mentally disturbed" daughter.

LOLA: I was alone. All alone in the world and this girl she was my friend. In the camp. Two people couldn't be closer. We helped each other get through each day and each night. Every morning we woke up was a triumph. We filled the time with talk, me and my little friend Anna. We told each other stories about what *was* and what *will* be. □□□ What stories she told! You know the expression "like an artist"? She painted pictures with words. □□□ You had a perfect picture in your head of everything she described. You knew what all the faces looked like, every member of her family, her cat, the boy she wanted to marry, Peter. "Anna, you tell such wonderful stories," I told her. □□□ "You should be a writer." And she told me, □□□ "I *am* a writer. As a matter of fact, I've written a whole book." "What kind of book," I asked, "does such a young girl write?" And she told me, "A book of ideas and observations, ideas about life. A kind of a diary," she said. "And where *is* this diary of yours," I asked my young friend. And she smiled. "You'll see, one day you'll see." And I didn't think anything of it except her black eyes twinkled in such a way I can see them right now. And then I said to her, "Well, why don't you keep a book *here*, here in the camp?" And she said, □□□ "Lola, what a good idea, I can't thank you enough." So, thanks to me, all the time we were at Belsen, she secretly kept a book. A diary, another diary. Where she found the paper to write on I'll never know. Whatever she could get her hands on. Little scraps, rags. She wrote things down all the time. Whenever you saw her, she was jotting something down. All day long. She'd be too weak to eat, but there was Anna, writing. In plain sight, writing. Finally I had to say something. "Anna, what's with all the writing? The guards are gonna find out and murder you." And do you know what she said to me? □□□ "I don't care *what* happens to me," she said. "I may not survive the war but I must write down everything, everything I see and everything I feel. All I care about is people should see what I write and know the truth and remember. I want people to remember." She kept on writing, right till the end. Sometimes she was too starved to keep her head up but I held it up for her so she could write. When she got too sick—typhus she had—too sick to hold even a matchstick to write with, *I* wrote for her, I took dictation from Anna Frank. *(A beat)* As you would imagine, I was a big character in this book. I was the hero— □□□ The heroine. Well, it was *her* book, true, but I was there, on every single page. "Lola did *this*," or "Lola said *this* today." "Lola gives me the strength to go on." "Lola has such courage." Can you imagine? *Me*, Lola, I gave Anna Frank the will to live may she rest in peace. □□□ When she died in my arms, and I'll never forget it as long as I live, she made me promise: "Hide my book, Lola." Her voice was weak, I had to bend my ear close. "Don't let them take it," she said. "Make sure people read what I wrote, people should know. Promise me, Lola, promise me." I promised. And little Anna Frank smiled, and closed her eyes and she was gone, right in my arms. *(Becoming choked up)* I did the best I could. I tried to save it. It was my story. I promised Anna. I kept it hidden. Every day I lived in fear. I trusted no one. If only the Nazis didn't find it and piss all over it. □□□ If only that book lasted through the war. . . . I'm telling you, I was the heroine, it was my story. She wrote about *me*! I could've given people hope. But my story, *Lola*'s story, told by Anne Frank, went up in flames with her at Belsen. The Belsen diary. The *other* diary. The diary nobody knows about. The diary *I* told her to keep. □□□ But who knew this little girl, the young friend I gave my crumbs to, my little sister, who *I* inspired, who knew what she would become? This girl with black eyes writing, writing all the time. Who knew what she would mean to the world? Just a girl, but a magical girl. Her name was Anna. Anna Frank from Amsterdam. Yes. The same. *(A beat)* Years go by. Our boat comes into New York in fog so thick, I never got to see the Statue of Liberty. Then. One day, in Brooklyn, in my kitchen, on Beverley Road, I see in *Life* magazine a story about a diary found in Amsterdam, and a picture, a picture of a girl with eyes like black marbles and I say, Anna! You said to me, "One day you'll see!" Anna, my little friend! *(A beat)* And that is the story of me and Anne Frank.

MY BRAZIL

BY RACHEL ROSENTHAL

"We had lived in Brazil seven months," writes Rachel Rosenthal in this autobiographical "recital," which she has also performed. "During that time I died, I was born, I was weaned, reimprinted and bonded for good. I may even have been dwarfed and bonsaied too. I don't know if I ever grew up." She was thirteen years old at the time her parents fled with her to South America to escape the Nazi takeover of France; less that a year later, when the Nazi menace threatened Jews living in Brazil, they emigrated to New York. My Brazil, *written many decades later, recollects in song, dance and speech the ripe details of that time and place.*

When I lived in Tarzana, just before the events that led to my leaving home, I was swimming in our pool one day, when I happened to look up at the sky. Way up there, very high and very small, was what I later recognized to be a white sheet of paper, waltzing and zigzagging in air currents, ascending, descending, dancing its gradual approach to earth. For some reason, I couldn't take my eyes off it, and it became a kite, with my gaze the string it was attached to. And I reeled it in, slowly but surely, until that piece of paper fluttered down into the pool beside me, within two feet of where I was standing! I felt singled out somehow, and vaguely heard a call, but didn't recognize the voice.

A long time ago, a similar event took place.

I was with my parents, high above Rio de Janeiro, at the base of the forty-foot Christ on top of Corcovado mountain. It was in 1940. Some new friends took us sightseeing in their car. It was just before the rainy season and the sky was stridently clear. As I was walking around the big statue, I was eyeing uneasily a huge, jet black butterfly flapping about in the hot, still air. I had a butterfly phobia. Suddenly, a gust of wind swept him away in the direction of the sea. I looked out at the string of sparkling bays in the white-hot sun under the cycloramic blue sky. And then I saw a black cloud, like a tiny spot on the horizon. The air around us began to churn. The black butterfly was whirled back as I watched that speck of black cloud racing toward us at vertiginous speed, progressively blotting out the blue of sky, until it was all around us, the wind howling, huge raindrops pelting us as we ran for the car and as the black butterfly fought for balance trying to reach the shelter of the jungle growth. We raced down the mountain road, but by the time we reached bottom there was an ocher-colored flood in the streets and our car fairly floated.

I know today but didn't know it then, that I had died as I am dying now. I was also born then, in Brazil, in 1940. This corpse was born in Rio, age thirteen, the product of a cosmic upheaval and a very private alchemy.

MARISOL

BY JOSÉ RIVERA

Marisol is killed, pumped with hundreds of rounds of machine-gun fire. She is a casualty of the earth's destruction and of the angels' rebellion against God, now crashing to an end in the war-torn heavens. This speech ends the play. Marisol is isolated onstage, in separate light. Elsewhere, the city's homeless throw rocks at the sky, a small moon appears far away, and, finally, an angel appears beside Marisol, holding a gold crown, a sign of triumph and new hope.

MARISOL: I'm killed instantly. Little blazing lead meteors enter my body. My blood cells ride those bullets into outer space. My soul surges up the oceans of the Milky Way at the speed of light. At the moment of death, I see the invisible war. □□□ Thousands of years of fighting pass in an instant. New and terrible forms of warfare, monstrous weapons, and unimagined strains of terror are created and destroyed in billionths of a second. Galaxies spring from a single drop of angel's sweat while hundreds of armies fight and die on the fingertips of children in the Bronx. □□□

Three hundred million million beautiful angels die in the first charge of the Final Battle. The oceans are salty with rebel blood. Angels drop like lightning from the dying sky. The rebels are in full retreat. There's chaos. There's blood and fire and ambulances and Heaven's soldiers scream and fight and die in beautiful, beautiful light. It looks like the revolution is doomed □□□ then, as if one body, one mind, the innocent of the earth take to the streets with anything they can find—rocks, sticks, screams—and aim their displeasure at the senile sky and fire into the tattered wind on the side of the angels . . . billions of poor, of homeless, of peaceful, of silent, of angry . . . fighting and fighting as no species has ever fought before. Inspired by the earthly noise, the rebels advance! □□□

New ideas rip the Heavens. New powers are created. New miracles are signed into law. It's the first day of the new history. □□□

Oh god. What light. What possibilities. What hope.

FURTHER READING

At TCG we have been honored to work with the following writers to provide a permanent home for their art in book form. We urge you to explore further these exceptional artists.

JON ROBIN BAITZ
The End of Day and *The Film Society* from *The Substance of Fire and Other Plays*, copyright ©1993.

Three Hotels from *Three Hotels: Plays and Monologues*, copyright ©1994.

ERIC BOGOSIAN
Talk Radio from *The Essential Bogosian*, copyright ©1994.

LAURIE CARLOS, JESSICA HAGEDORN AND ROBBIE MCCAULEY
Teenytown from *Out from Under: Texts by Women Performance Artists*, copyright ©1988, 1989 and 1990.

LENORA CHAMPAGNE
Getting Over Tom from *Out from Under: Texts by Women Performance Artists*, copyright ©1982.

CONSTANCE CONGDON
No Mercy from *Tales of the Lost Formicans and Other Plays*, copyright ©1994.

E. L. DOCTOROW
Drinks Before Dinner, copyright ©1978 and 1979.

RICHARD FOREMAN
Film Is Evil; Radio Is Good from *Unbalancing Acts: Foundations for a Theater*, copyright ©1992, published by arrangement with Random House, Inc.

REYNOLDS PRICE
Early Dark from *Full Moon and Other Plays*, copyright ©1993.

AISHAH RAHMAN
The Mojo and the Sayso from *Moon Marked and Touched by Sun*, copyright ©1991.

RONALD RIBMAN
Buck from *The Rug Merchants of Chaos and Other Plays*, copyright ©1992.

JOSÉ RIVERA
Cloud Tectonics and *Marisol* from *Marisol and Other Plays*, copyright ©1997.

RACHEL ROSENTHAL
My Brazil from *Out from Under: Texts by Women Performance Artists*, copyright ©1979 and 1990.

BEATRICE ROTH
The Father from *Out from Under: Texts by Women Performance Artists*, copyright ©1985 and 1990.

MILCHA SANCHEZ-SCOTT
Roosters from *On New Ground: Contemporary Hispanic-American Plays*, copyright ©1987.

NICKY SILVER
Fat Men in Skirts and *The Food Chain* from *Etiquette and Vitriol: The Food Chain and Other Plays*, copyright ©1996.

Raised in Captivity, copyright ©1995.

STEPHEN SONDHEIM, GEORGE FURTH AND HAL PRINCE
Company, copyright ©1996.

DANITRA VANCE
Live and in Color! from *Moon Marked and Touched by Sun*, copyright ©1991 and 1994.

The following list provides contact information regarding performance rights to the work included in this volume:

Jon Robin Baitz c/o George Lane, William Morris Agency, 1325 Ave. of the Americas, NY NY 10019; Eric Bogosian c/o George Lane, William Morris Agency, 1325 Ave. of the Americas, NY NY 10019; Laurie Carlos, Jessica Hagedorn, Robbie McCauley c/o Harold Schmidt Literary Agency, 342 W. 12th St., NY NY 10014; Lenora Champagne c/o TCG; Constance Congdon c/o William Morris Agency, 1325 Ave. of the Americas, NY NY 10019; E. L. Doctorow c/o Amanda Urban, International Creative Management, 40 W. 57th St., NY NY 10019; George Furth c/o The Lantz Agency, 888 7th Ave., NY NY 10036; David Greenspan c/o TCG; Tina Howe c/o Flora Roberts, Inc., 157 W. 57th St., NY NY 10019; Holly Hughes c/o Grove/Atlantic Inc., 841 Broadway, NY NY 10003; David Henry Hwang c/o Writers and Artists Agency, 19 W. 44th St., Suite 1000, NY NY 10036; Adam P. and Adrienne Kennedy c/o Joyce Ketay Agency, 1501 Broadway, Suite 1908, NY NY 10036; Harry Kondoleon c/o George Lane, William Morris Agency, 1325 Ave. of the Americas, NY NY 10019; Tony Kushner c/o Joyce Ketay Agency, 1501 Broadway, Suite 1908, NY NY 10036; Romulus Linney c/o Peregrine Whittlesey Agency 345 E. 80th St., #31F, NY NY 10021; Craig Lucas c/o Peter Franklin, William Morris Agency, 1325 Ave. of the Americas, NY NY 10019; Eduardo Machado c/o TCG; Emily Mann c/o George Lane, William Morris Agency, 1325 Ave. of the Americas, NY NY 10019; Donald Margulies c/o Rosenstone / Wender, 3 E. 48th St., NY NY 10017; Marsha Norman c/o The Tantleff Agency, 375 Greenwich St., Suite 603, NY NY 10013; John O'Keefe c/o TCG; Suzan-Lori Parks c/o George Lane, William Morris Agency, 1325 Ave. of the Americas, NY NY 10019; Reynolds Price c/o TCG; Aishah Rahman c/o TCG; Ronald Ribman c/o Flora Roberts, Inc, 157 W. 57th St., NY NY 10019; José Rivera c/o Joyce Ketay Agency, 1501 Broadway, Suite 1908, NY NY 10036; Rachel Rosenthal c/o TCG; Beatrice Roth c/o TCG; Milcha Sanchez-Scott c/o George Lane, William Morris Agency, 1325 Ave. of the Americas, NY NY 10019; Nicky Silver c/o George Lane, William Morris Agency, 1325 Ave. of the Americas, NY NY 10019; Stephen Sondheim c/o Flora Roberts Inc., 157 W. 57th St., NY NY 10019; DanitraVance c/o William Morris Agency, 1325 Ave. of the Americas, NY NY 10019; Paula Vogel c/o Peter Franklin, William Morris Agency, 1325 Ave. of the Americas, NY NY 10019; John Weidman c/o TCG.

TODD LONDON is the artistic director of New Dramatists, the country's oldest center for the support and development of playwrights. A former managing editor of *American Theatre* magazine and the author of *The Artistic Home*, published by Theatre Communications Group, he recently served as guest literary director of the American Repertory Theatre and visiting lecturer of dramatic arts at Harvard. He writes regularly about the arts for *American Theatre, The Village Voice*, and others. In 1993–94, he was senior writer on *Theatre in America*, a five-part documentary series in development for Great Performances, WNET/Thirteen in New York. He was an assistant professor of drama at New York University's Tisch School of the Arts from 1990–94. He has chaired the New York State Council on the Arts theatre panel and served as associate artistic director of New York's Classic Stage Company. In 1997, his writing for *American Theatre* magazine, including his three-part series "Open Call: A Year in the Lives of 15 Actors Starting Out in New York," garnered him the George Jean Nathan Award for dramatic criticism.